PARTNERING

Sidra Stone

Hal Stone

PARTNERING

A NEW KIND OF RELATIONSHIP

HAL STONE, PH.D. & SIDRA L. STONE, PH.D.

NATARAJ PUBLISHING
a division of

NEW WORLD LIBRARY
NOVATO, CALIFORNIA

NATARAJ PUBLISHING
a division of

NEW WORLD LIBRARY
14 PAMARON WAY
NOVATO, CALIFORNIA 94949

Edited by Gina Misiroglu
Front cover design by Peri Poloni
Art direction and text design by Mary Ann Casler

The authors of this book do not dispense medical advice or prescribe the use
of any technique as a form of treatment for physical or mental problems
without the advice of a physician, either directly or indirectly. In the event you
use any of the information in this book, neither the authors nor the publisher
can assume any responsibility for your actions. The intent of the authors is to
offer information of a general nature to help your quest for personal growth.

Library of Congress Cataloging-in-Publication Data
Stone, Hal.
Partnering : a new kind of relationship : how to love each other without
losing yourselves / by Hal Stone and Sidra L. Stone
p.   cm.
ISBN 1-57731-107-8 (alk. paper)
1. Man-woman relationships. 2. Interpersonal relations. 3. Intimacy
(Psychology) I. Stone, Sidra, 1937– II. Title.
HQ801.S845 2000
306.7–dc21   99-049353
First Printing, January 2000
ISBN 1-57731-107-8
Printed in Canada on acid-free paper
Distributed to the trade by Publishers Group West

10 9 8 7 6 5 4 3 2 1

To Lisa and Little Harry,
who started it all

CONTENTS

SECTION 2
Enhancing Relationship

Chapter 6
Passionate Partnering: Sexuality and
Sensuality beyond the Bedroom 139

Chapter 7
Partnering As a Business Venture:
Learning to Share the Details of Life 167

Chapter 8
Partnering and Parenting:
A Couple's Guide to Romance 181

Chapter 9
The Top Ten Challenges to Relationship:
Keeping Your Love Alive Amid Life's Routines 197

Chapter 10
Partners on the Path: Spirituality and Partnering 217

INTRODUCTION

This book is about relationship. The basic ideas that we are presenting apply to all relationships, but our emphasis is on primary relationships where two people are living together over time. Many of us grew up believing that the idea of love was very simple. You met someone and fell in love and if love was present then that was all that was necessary for a great relationship. You lived happily ever after. At least this was the fairy-tale fantasy that many people bought into. But we have noticed that this is not how it is in the real world. Although love is very important to most people, it alone will not do the job of preserving relationship. You need love and you need a commitment to working toward personal growth for yourselves and for the relationship as well. The personal work gives you the means to deal with the amazing variety of challenges that can destroy love, and the love gives you the magical elixir that makes all the work worthwhile.

It would be unreal to expect all primary relationships to remain together forever. Although we know this, it is still painful to us to watch relationships disintegrate amid great pain and suffering. This is particularly true when the two partners concerned have no understanding of a few fundamental principles of relationship. This book is about these basic ideas and principles. It is our honest feeling that, when they are understood and put into use, they can make a real difference in people's lives.

The issue for us, however, is not whether or not a particular relationship remains intact. For us the primary issue is learning to recognize that any relationship can be a teacher once you know how to take advantage of the teachings it brings. This idea of "relationship as teacher" is very basic to our approach and in our view it can be deeply healing to the process of relationship. When used this way relationship can become a path to emotional and spiritual growth that is extraordinary in its scope and depth.

Since we first met many years ago, relationship has been our primary teacher. Our discovery of the many selves that live within each of us was a personal and relational revolution for both of us. Nevertheless, like every other couple we know, we had to learn about relationship by living it, by tripping over ourselves and getting up over and over again, and, most of all, by always recognizing that we were truly teachers for each other.

For many years we struggled with the conflict between surrendering to another person and maintaining our own separate identities. What finally became clear to us was that the idea of surrender in relationship is not to another *person* but to the *process of relationship* itself. We learned to trust that our relationship would take us exactly where we needed to go. As we learned to trust this process and as we did the work with ourselves and with each other that the process required, we learned that this kind of surrender required a great deal of work on both of our parts. It is our hope that our ideas will make your own path a little bit easier.

We are passionate advocates of relationship. We do not believe that the magic in relationship must die when people get married or when they have children. This happens with alarming frequency because so many people are following old patterns of behavior and old rules. They need to learn how to make their relationships work in the world as it is today. Fortunately there are more and more teachers who are writing about how to have successful relationships. We salute their work.

In this book we propose a new way to be in relationship that builds on the successes of the past and adds in a great deal that is new in order to deal with the realities of the present. This kind of relationship is one in which two people are partners to each other. We think of this kind of partnering as a "joint venture." It moves beyond the automatic acceptance of (or even the automatic rejection of) traditional roles and the personalities that fulfilled these roles. It emphasizes cooperation and equality, mutual respect, and mutual empowerment. It also involves looking at your relationship in a new, completely "no-fault" way that, once you learn it, will give you great clarity. It invites complexity and depth and it uses your relationship as a vehicle for healing and growth. Last, but certainly not least, it can make your relationship more passionate and much more fun!

Over the years we have worked with a very large number of people. We have learned a great deal from them and from their relationships. We have also learned priceless lessons from our own relationship and the relationships with our children, stepchildren, and grandchildren. We have discovered some very basic facts that make understanding relationships easier and some fairly simple strategies for making relationships better. At this point in our lives we have a pretty good idea of what works and what does not work. Our book brings you a distillation of our experience.

There is a practical side to relationship, but there is magic as well. Much of this book is devoted to teaching you the practical material. Most of all, however, we hope that you will rediscover, or discover for the first time, the magic, excitement, and power of the relationships in your life. It is also our hope that love and consciousness will be your constant companions as you sail through the charted and uncharted seas of relationship.

— Hal and Sidra Stone
Albion, California

PARTNERING

SECTION 1

A NEW WAY OF LOOKING AT PARTNERING

The No-Fault Relationship

Chapter 1

RELATIONSHIP AS A JOINT VENTURE

Each of us has our own special basket that contains the magic of who we are and what we hold most precious in life. When we first meet and fall in love we get a glimpse into, and a feeling for, the interior world of our partner. We inhale the fragrance and magic of the other's essential being. Then come the problems of life and one day, sometimes sooner and sometimes later, the magic is gone.

We would like to begin this book by telling you the story of "The Star Maiden." We read this wonderful Bushman tale in Sir Laurens van der Post's book *The Heart of the Hunter* and it is one of our favorite stories. We feel that it provides a beautifully haunting introduction to this book and to our picture of partnering as a "joint venture" relationship.

Once upon a time there was a Bushman who raised cows on a farm in the Kalahari Desert. His life was serene and simple but lonely. One morning when he went out to milk his cows, he saw that they had already been milked. He couldn't imagine who had done this. The next morning when he came out he found again that the cows had been milked during the night.

The next night the Bushman resolved to hide in a shed near the cows in order to discover who had been milking them. As midnight approached he saw a remarkable sight. Climbing down from heaven on a ladder that extended between the stars and the earth was a multitude of Star Maidens. Their beauty took his breath away. Each Star Maiden carried a bucket and as she touched down onto his land, she began to milk his cows. The Star Maidens milked the cows all night long and as the dawn approached they began their trip back to the stars, ascending the ladder one by one. The farmer could not bear to see them leave. Just as the last Star Maiden approached the ladder, he darted out from his hiding place, took her by the hand, and begged her to become his wife. Surprising though it was, the magical Star Maiden was happy to marry the simple farmer.

When they returned to the farmhouse, the Star Maiden told him the following: "I am delighted to marry you and I promise you that your farm will prosper. I have only one condition that I must set. I have here a basket. You must promise me never to open this basket. If you do open it, then I will be forced to leave you." The farmer promised that he would do as she wished. The Star Maiden put her basket down in a corner of the room, and so their life together began.

As his new wife promised, the farmer's farm and crops prospered and he became one of the most successful farmers in the whole area. His wife went out into the fields to work every day and everything that she touched seemed blessed by the gods. He was a very happy man and, as the years passed, he became happier yet with his good fortune, for he loved and appreciated the Star Maiden.

One afternoon when his wife was out in the fields and he was at home looking for something, he found the basket she had put away many years before. Though he remembered the injunction of his wife, he didn't take it seriously any longer so he picked up the basket, put it on the table, and opened it up. To his surprise he found it empty. He found this very amusing and had a good laugh over the fact that it was empty. He remembered well the seriousness with which she had warned him about not opening her treasure.

A short time later the Star Maiden returned from the field. As she entered the room she knew immediately what had happened. She spoke to her husband with the following words: "A long time ago I warned you never to open up this basket because it was very special to me. I told you also that I would have to leave if you did open it. Well, you violated your oath and this evening I am going to be leaving you. I want you to understand the reason for this. I am not leaving you because you opened up this basket without my permission. That would have been all right after all these years. I am leaving you because when you opened the basket you found nothing in it. That is why I can no longer be with you."

And so it was that as night came the Star Maiden, with great sadness, climbed the ladder back to her home in the sky, not because the farmer had broken his vow, but because *he had looked into her most precious possession and could see nothing there.* This basket contained the Star Maiden's essence. When he looked into her basket, he had looked into the depths of her soul, at the magic she had brought with her to this earth from her home in the stars. He had looked, but he had seen nothing. He was blind to her magic, and the Star Maiden could no longer stay with him.

Isn't this really how it is so often in relationship? Each of us has our own special basket that contains the magic of who we are and what we hold most precious in life. When we first meet and fall in love we get a glimpse into, and a feeling for, the interior world of our partner and we inhale the fragrance and magic of the other's essential being. Then come the problems of life. We feel pressured to succeed, to make more money, to push harder. We have children who begin to carry the magic and we have less and less of it with one another. One day, sometimes sooner and sometimes later, the magic is gone. When we look into the basket, it is empty and we feel hurt, disappointed, and bewildered. The relationship is over even though we may live with one another for the remainder of our lives.

Despite many claims to the contrary, this magic does *not* have to disappear. Keeping the magic requires some effort, however. We must be willing to learn the lessons that relationship has to teach us. We must also be willing to take time to nourish the connection that exists between our partners and ourselves. All this is possible. This book is about keeping the magic — and the excitement — alive in your relationship.

Believe it or not, it is possible to keep this magic alive. We have built our lives together upon this belief, and are living proof that a relationship can more than endure over time, it can blossom. But you need to give it the right kind of attention, and you need a certain willingness to commit to the unfolding of your relationship and to the idea of using it as a teacher. The following pages outline some of the fundamental truths that are necessary to successful partnerships, as well as the core principles of fulfilling relationships. They are born out of years of our working with couples, and constitute what we believe to be the very building blocks of an emotionally healthy, sexually fulfilling harmony. You'll find that these ideas are interwoven at various levels throughout the book; they provide both the framework for the book and the framework for thriving relationships.

LOVE AND THE MUTUAL
EXPLORATION OF CONSCIOUSNESS

As you can tell from the story of "The Star Maiden," we are a pair of incurable romantics. But we have discovered that romance is not enough. So, we use the term *joint venture* to describe a new kind of relationship in which two people come together for not only love, romance, and sexual chemistry, but also partnership, personal growth, and spiritual evolution. *Love alone cannot make a relationship work because the forces that can destroy love are too powerful and, for most of us, too unconscious.* Mutual exploration, learning, and personal growth without love cannot do the job either, because love is the oil, the elixir, that soothes everything and makes it all worthwhile.

So, what does this mean? It means that, according to the first principle of partnership, you must have both love and a commitment to the mutual exploration of consciousness in order to convert your relationship to a partnering model. We cannot tell you how many times in our earlier years together that we reached a point where we both feared our love was dead. We felt utterly defeated and saddened and frustrated that the end had come. Then we did some work with each other. Hal may have shared negative reactions he had been harboring toward Sidra that he hadn't been aware of. Sidra may have realized that they both were overworked or that she was giving too much energy to her family. Or a dream may have come that clarified what had been going on unconsciously. Suddenly the love returned, in full force and even more powerful than before, because we had mastered a new experience. After we saw this happen hundreds of times in our clients and ourselves, we realized the power of this combination of love and mutual exploration. This is why we scoff at people who insist that passion and romance must die with marriage and children. Romance dies because people don't have any kind of systematic way to deal with the host of things that impact marriage in a negative way. That is why the exploration of consciousness is a process that must go on forever.

We are not suggesting that all partners will be together forever. It often happens that the process of relationship can lead people to separate. What we can say is that the vast majority of relationships end because people don't know how to handle the negativity and the sense of being overwhelmed that so easily invades primary relationships.

PARTNERING VERSUS
HIERARCHICAL RELATIONSHIP

The second basic principle of partnering is that there is a fundamental equality between the partners. This kind of partnering is nonhierarchical. Each partner may have strengths and weaknesses in relationship to the other (for instance, one may be good with the big picture and the other may be good with the details), but these differences are seen as a way to augment and help support each other. Achieving this fundamental equality is more easily said than done because such a shift requires us to examine our basic power motives in our dealings with people. As each of us came to our relationship accustomed to being the person in charge, we can assure you that the ability to come to this equality with each other was not easy, but the rewards have been well worth the effort.

Most relationships exist in a hierarchical form. What this means is that people either adopt a role of wielding power over someone weaker or of being submissive to someone who is more powerful. This classical hierarchical relationship is what creates the "bonding patterns" that have contributed so much to our understanding of relationships. In its simplest form, *bonding patterns* is a term that describes the parent-child interactions we learned as children that automatically govern our relationships until we become aware of them. These bonding patterns can be positive or negative. (For more discussion of bonding patterns, see chapter 3.)

Hierarchical relationships are often related to family and cultural training that establishes rules about how we should behave in relationship. (For more discussion of hierarchical relationships, see Sidra's book, *The Shadow King: The Invisible Force That Holds Women Back*.) For more and more couples, however, this traditional hierarchical structure no longer works.

Most of us yearn for a more equal partnership and a deeper and more fulfilling kind of relationship. To achieve this, however, we must address our traditional hierarchical training. Most of us need to spend a good deal of time learning to recognize how these ideas and behavior patterns live within us and color our system of relationships. When we recognize and understand these, we have the freedom to accept or reject them as we see fit.

Once we have tasted partnering, particularly in primary relationship, we simply cannot have any other kind of connection. Partnering moves us into a relationship that is truly a *joint venture,* a venture that takes us into spiritual realms even as it helps us to deal with the myriad practical details of everyday living. A joint venture relationship can exist whether the partners are of the same sex or opposite sexes. Partnering is partnering and the same psychic laws apply to all of us.

In the business world, if two very different people start a business as a joint venture, they are equal partners. The success or failure of the business will depend to a great extent on their ability to function as equal partners. The same thing is true in partnering relationships of all kinds. Although many of us would prefer this joint venture kind of connection in our business and personal relationships, life has a way of messing things up and what begins as a very positive system of interactions between equals can easily turn into murkiness and negativity or outright war.

It is one thing to want a true partnering in our relationships. It is another thing to know how to get it and keep it. This takes work and learning and an attitude toward relationship that is radically different from anything that has been available in the past. In the following chapters we talk about how your partnering can go sour so easily. You'll learn why this happens, what this is all about, and what you can do about it.

PRINCIPLES OF SUCCESSFUL PARTNERING

The skills we must learn for successful partnering require us to explore areas of knowledge and experience that may be completely new to us. Some of this knowledge is based on what our minds can handle. Some learning has to do with the development of a knowing heart. Other insights are based on — what to our minds are nonexistent — matters of the spirit. Still other knowledge comes from our physical bodies. Once we enter into the adventure of real partnering, we begin to explore all of these areas because each has its own secrets and these secrets impact our interactions with other people. Let's look at some of the learning that a joint venture relationship requires of us.

Discovering the Reality of the Many Selves and How They Interact

You can learn about relationship from many wonderful teachers, writers, and therapists. When it comes to learning about the *psychology of selves* and their interaction in relationship, however, our work is the primary source.

From our perspective there is nothing that is more important, more vital, more helpful, or more essential than the realization that we have within us a group of selves that regulates our lives and directs our actions, even though we think that our choices come from free will.

Put another way: *Without the knowledge of one's inner selves there is little possibility for truly rewarding and successful relationships.* Why is this so? It is so because a relationship is not something that exists between two people. Any relationship involves a multitude of selves in each person that interact with similar or opposite selves in the other. We have to learn *who* in us is interacting with our partner at any particular time.

As a man, I (Hal) discovered that I had been leading a life that was dominated by a particular self that had to do with being responsible. This often forced me to do things that I really did not want to do. When we are identified with a particular self we have no choice about our behavior. It is automatic. And when we do things automatically it is not healthy for us or for our partners, because often we become resentful without consciously recognizing it at the time. We *can* change this, however. In order to do so, we must learn to recognize the selves that run our lives and separate from them. Then we can choose to use their expertise in a conscious way. For instance, when the responsible father within Hal happily and automatically wants to give up an enjoyable afternoon at the gym in order to help Sidra around the house, Hal takes some time to see what the more self-nurturing parts of him would have to say about this. Then, instead of automatically staying home — and later resenting this decision — he is able to consider the alternative of not helping her. Hal has a real choice; his responsible father self does not.

Balancing the Process of Primary Relationship with Individual Choice and Freedom

To surrender in partnering does not mean surrendering to your partner or to another person. It means to surrender to the *process* of relationship that develops when two people commit to one another. This process of relationship becomes the third party. Incidentally, this surrender is not necessarily a commitment to either monogamy or non-monogamy. Neither is it a guarantee that the relationship will remain forever intact. It is simply the recognition that the process of the relationship is a third and separate entity that has a life of its own.

If you surrender to the process of primary relationship then you must learn to listen to your partner. This does not mean that you must obey or agree with your partner, just that you must truly listen and feel your partner's reality. If you cannot listen or you do not hear what your partner is trying to say, then you must find out why this is so. Why can't you hear what your partner is trying to tell you? What stops this from happening? You must continually give energy to the process of relationship and do whatever is necessary to move through the roadblocks that inevitably develop between partners.

It is not easy to find a balance between this surrender to the process of relationship and your need to feel and behave like an independent human being. If you do something that goes contrary to the requirements of your partner, you must learn to understand the viewpoint and feel the pain of your partner. You must carry both of your realities, yours and your partner's. You cannot just fly off into rebellion or power to prove that you are tough and strong and independent as you go off to "do your thing."

The key here is that each of us must learn to feel our own vulnerability so that we can feel the vulnerability of our partners. This deepens connections. Embracing our vulnerability is a very threatening thing to do in relationship because it means meeting the other person without defenses. To learn to live with our vulnerability in an emotionally healthy way is to learn to live in relationship in an undefended way. This does not mean that we give up our power and become victims; it just means that we must feel our vulnerability.

Relationship As a Business Venture

We find ourselves in awe of the complexity of life these days. We do not know what it was like in earlier times, but this complexity seems to have risen exponentially since the industrial revolution. When we combine two lives, add in children and family and friends and the technological revolution we are in, it can feel as though each of us is running a giant business corporation.

It is important to recognize that life is very complex and the details of relationship are also complex. It helps to recognize, as early as possible, that a primary relationship is not just a personal adventure but also a major business venture that involves an enormous number of details. If you do not take the business side seriously, these details begin to erode the intimacy of the personal connection and the magic disappears.

There is an excellent analogy to computers that can help you to see this point. Computers have a number of default settings that simplify their use. For example, the type of print and the type size are set up so that whenever you start to work this default position automatically opens. You can change it if you want, but it is quite automatic and saves you a good deal of time. Otherwise, there are a multitude of settings to see to every time you begin to work.

In a similar fashion, if partners do not *consciously* decide who is going to handle what in the multitude of tasks that face them, then a default position goes into operation and the partners do things not out of conscious choice but rather out of old habit patterns. So, if a woman has been a very responsible person from her earliest years, she will, by default, take on more and more responsibility for more and more things until she is eaten up by details. The woman that she was in the beginning of the partnership easily dies in this way as she drowns in obligations and requirements that, at a deeper level, she resents. Imagine that her partner is used to his mother taking care of all of his needs. His default position is to view a wife as someone who is there to take care of his needs much as his mother did. This causes no end of trouble because the early family patterns are transferred onto the new relationship and this ultimately creates serious problems.

One of the wonderful things about relationship is that partners have different strengths and weaknesses. Each person brings into relationship a unique set of values, sensibilities, experience, and knowledge and many of these are complementary. So it is that one person's strength can be another person's weakness. If used properly, this is one of the great gifts of partnering. Partners can "rest into" each other and allow the partner with a specific strength to handle the main responsibility for that particular area of life. The idea of "resting into" means using these differences in a conscious way and not allowing the default position to determine what each partner does. Consciously resting into someone is very different from *unconsciously* allowing that person to take over a particular area of expertise.

For example, in our relationship Sidra has historically had the primary responsibility for keeping our finances in order. On a regular basis, however, we talk over the finances so Hal knows what is happening. If we do not do this, then when things go wrong Hal can easily become irritable and angry (we would say that a self that is irritable and angry takes over) because he has abdicated financial responsibility to Sidra, or Sidra may become resentful about carrying the entire burden.

On the other side, Hal has had the primary responsibility for setting up the teaching and travel schedule. Sidra is apprised of these activities and no final decision is ever made without her participation. So, she rests into Hal in this area without abdicating responsibility just as Hal rests into her expertise on the finances without abdicating responsibility.

To deal with the myriad of issues that partners must handle, it is necessary to honor the business side of life and relationship and make clear choices in partnership about what belongs to each person at any given time. This may change by the week, month, or year but it must be attended to.

Understanding the Role of Judgment and Self-Criticism in Relationships

For most people it is relatively easy to fall in love. Sadly enough, it is even easier for this love to be destroyed. To create a successful relationship, you must understand the issues that destroy love and develop the ability to partner with another person so that together you can combat the destructive forces and overcome them.

Certainly understanding judgment is a major key to success in partnering. There are two kinds of judgments. One is the kind of judgment we make toward someone else. The other is the judgment we make toward ourselves. This last is commonly known as self-criticism and is based on what we call the *inner critic,* a self that lives inside of us and just loves to say nasty things about us. Both of these have a devastating effect on partnering. (For more on the inner critic, see our book *Embracing Your Inner Critic.*)

A judgment toward another person can be silent or spoken. If you do not like something your partner does or says and you say nothing, this unspoken reaction becomes a judgment inside of you and distances you from your partner. After this happens ten times or a hundred times, you relate to your partner in a totally different way. You lose yourself and your love dissipates as a more judgmental self in you takes over. When this happens, you find yourself looking at your partner critically and judging him or her either silently or out loud. Soon your partner begins to feel that you are acting like a judgmental parent. Actually, to our way of thinking, you are.

What generally happens in partnering is that one person carries the judgments and the other person becomes the receiver of, even the victim of, these judgments. The victims in partnering are usually self-critical. They can find nothing right about themselves and they usually come from family backgrounds where the family system was very harsh toward them. Connecting to someone who is very judgmental is a natural, and painful, outgrowth of such an early development.

Strong self-criticism is devastating to partnership as well because the other partner is forced into a role. As the other partner, you either have to keep building up your partner, which gets very dull after a while, or you begin to get angry. When this happens it is easy to become judgmental and, before you know it, you are drawn into a role that you never really wanted to be in. You are your partner's judge.

Please note that when we speak of judgments in relationship, we are speaking about ordinary judgments, not abuse. There are relationships that are abusive. We are not suggesting that you remain in an abusive relationship so that you can learn the lessons that your partner's judgments might teach you. If you are in an abusive relationship, please seek therapy with an appropriate professional.

Learning about Vulnerability: The Agony and the Ecstasy

The other side of judgment is our vulnerability. This is probably the most important lesson there is in all partnering work. Learning to live with vulnerability is the agony. Enjoying the depth

ionship that it brings is the ecstasy. Why is vulnerability so
tant? Why do we say it is so much the crux of successful partnering?

We are born into the world as very vulnerable children. Our
whole personality essentially consists of ideas and behavior patterns that are trying to take care of our vulnerability and make us
safe in the world. If we are powerful, we feel less vulnerable. If we
become very responsible, we feel less vulnerable. If we are nice to
people and we please them, we feel less vulnerable. If we rebel
against authority that we feel is unfair to us, we feel less vulnerable. Judgment itself becomes an effective way of avoiding our vulnerability. Underlying every judgment is some fundamental issue of
vulnerability, some basic feeling of pain, helplessness, shyness, or
insecurity. No matter how much we know about these feelings, it
is always difficult to express them in relationship.

There are two steps to take in coming to grips with vulnerability. The first is to learn to feel it and to know that you have it. If
you are 100 percent identified with power, how can you feel your
vulnerability? Well, you can't. That is why one of the first steps in
partnering work is to recognize the selves that are running your life
and to learn how to separate from them. *Only when you begin to
separate from the power systems that sit on top of your vulnerability
can you begin to feel your vulnerability and reconnect to the magic
of your relationship.*

Once you learn to hear the music of vulnerability and to feel its
feelings, the next step is to learn how to communicate these feelings to your partner. We are not talking here about identifying with
vulnerability and becoming a victim. We are not talking about
becoming a weakling. What we are talking about is learning how
to communicate your vulnerability in relationship while at the same
time you are in touch with the parts of you that carry your strength.
This is one of the greatest — and most rewarding — challenges for
each and every one of us.

Learning Healthy Ways to Communicate and How to Be Heard

The basic principle of communication is a very simple one. It goes something like this: *"It's not what you say to your partner that is of central importance, but rather who in you is saying it!"*

People spend a great deal of time learning how to talk to one another and there is always a place for this kind of work, particularly for people who have had little or no training in any kind of communication skills. They need to learn what to say and what not to say. They also need to learn what words to use; that is, how to say it.

What is generally overlooked is the fact that the ultimate success of your communication process depends upon which selves in you are actually talking. For this reason, we do very little teaching about *what* people should say to one another. Instead, we focus on helping people become sensitized to the quality of communication, the energy behind it. Because of this, in the chapters ahead we pay a great deal of attention to how your communications are received by your partner.

Learning the Importance of Sharing in Decision Making

Effective decision making depends on our understanding of the different selves that live in us. For example, if one partner is a power person and the other is very vulnerable, decision making is difficult even though, on the surface, it looks quite simple. The power person tends to hog the show and make all the decisions while the vulnerable partner feels overlooked and often becomes resentful or withdrawn. It is really difficult for love to last in a relationship like this.

There are other selves that pair up to make decision making really difficult. If one person is a power person who likes immediate action and the partner is a process person who loves to talk things over in detail, there may well be trouble. If one person is very parental and the other is fighting this authority by acting like a rebellious teenager, you can forget decision making because it isn't going to happen. Learning to recognize these different selves in our partners and ourselves and learning to appreciate that neither is right or wrong, just different, is the beginning of a very new and very different kind of communication.

Mastering the Energetic Connections in Relationship

In addition to the physical, emotional, mental, and spiritual connections of relationship, there is also an energetic connection, the basic premise of which is very simple: There is an energetic reality that exists and operates between yourself and others.

This area of energetic reality is one of our most exciting, juicy, and valuable discoveries since our original work with the psychology of selves. For us, this work with energetics has led to a redefining of intimacy that has had a great impact on the way that we "do" relationship and what we aspire to in relationship. The older idea of intimacy has to do with two people who are trying to come together and to blend their energies totally. This can lead to a kind of fusion and a loss of individuality. The new intimacy has to do with each of us having choice as to how we use our energetic connections with our partner. Instead of striving to always be close and blended with one another, this new goal is to have choice about how much to blend and how much we need to separate at any particular moment in time. The name that we give to this process of being together energetically is *energetic linkage*. The consequences of this mastery over the connections we make in our relationships are staggering. (For more discussion of energetic connections, see chapter 5.)

Embracing Sensuality and Sexuality

Many couples first become aware that their relationship is in trouble when they experience a sexual problem. As we have seen over and over again, when sexuality goes wrong, the relationship has also gone wrong in some way. Our experience has been that when fundamental relationship issues are cleared away, the sexual difficulties usually clear up of their own accord. If we cannot establish emotional intimacy in our relationships, then the sexuality usually suffers. This is why the discovery of which selves are running our personality has such a powerful effect on our ability to relate effectively to other people and why so many sexual areas get cleared up when we do our psychological homework.

In communication, the issue is not so much *what* we say to each other but rather *who* says it. In sexuality, the issue is not so much *what* partners are doing with each other as much as it is the question of *who* is it that is making the sexual connection. Learning about this helps us to get the right person (or self) out to do the job! (For more discussion of sensuality and sexuality, see chapter 6.)

It is important to establish a clear delineation between sensuality and sexuality. Sensual energy is what we often refer to as "Aphrodite energy." This kind of energy exists in both men and women, though in our experience women have a more natural connection to it. It is a very important kind of energy because it is empowering, it creates an intense experience of being alive, and it can provide a strong kind of connecting energy between two partners. It is quite surprising to learn how easy it is to be sexual and lack sensuality. When this sensuality is missing in relationship, you can have an active sexual connection and still feel sensually starved.

Sexuality has to do with the direct expression of our sexual impulses. It is focused upon genital sensation and direction. It can exist by itself without sensuality, or it can accompany sensuality. The experience of sexuality and sensuality is very different, and we demonstrate that difference as we explore these concepts more fully.

Including Children in Your Life without Giving up Your Primary Relationship

Many times we have asked partners when they felt their marriage had begun to unravel. And many times we have heard the same answer: "Our marriage ended, or began to deteriorate, when our first child was born."

Is primary relationship forever to be destroyed by the presence of children? The answer is — *very frequently* — yes, if partners don't do their homework. We have to discover the changes that occur with the birth of a child, how the whole network of energetic reality and linkage is changed. *The good news is that marriages can remain alive and vital if the work of relationship continues and if the children do not begin to occupy so much space that there is no longer any room for a truly alive, romantic partnering.* The energetic linkage in the partnership must be given priority even when children are involved or else a deterioration process will occur in the partnership and the primary linkage will go to the children, where it does not belong.

Because we are deeply committed to both primary relationships and children, we will be giving you many ideas in the coming chapters about how to combine parenting and partnering in a healthy and satisfying fashion, giving each the energy it deserves.

Meeting the Outside Challenges to Your Relationship

We have fantasies about writing a book on "how to destroy relationship" because showing what *not* to do can really get your attention. Until we write that book, however, we have taken the top ten challenges to relationships and gathered them together for you to see in chapter 9.

Your computer is one good example of the kind of challenge we're talking about. It is one thing to own and use a computer with some choice. It is another thing to be married to it so that it becomes the primary love object and you can no longer say no to it. The availability of the Internet and the possibility of immediate communication around the world can be very seductive.

Because of the many goodies that have been made available to us in the technological revolution, "things" can help to erode our connection to our partners. The fascination with cars, electronic devices, and so many other gadgets is always there to hook us, like a giant fishing line with delicious bait that is just waiting for us to bite into it. Going along with this is the stock market and the fascination with online investing and making more and more money. All of this can bring much pleasure to our lives and can even serve to enhance our relationships so long as we don't get hooked. The trick is to eat the bait and run!

Your Dream Life As a Mirror to Your Relationship

Dreams are very special to us and we want to give you some ideas about how to use them to enhance your relationship. They give us a picture of how the intelligence of the unconscious is responding to us individually and to our relationship collectively. Not everyone remembers dreams and we don't want you to think of this as an insurmountable problem because there are many ways to explore personal growth. If, however, you do remember your dreams, they can provide amazing opportunities for supporting the process of partnering.

Sometimes a dream is very objective and straightforward. A woman dreams three nights in a row that her husband is having an affair. She finally tells him the dream and asks for the truth and he finally discloses the affair to her. It is really quite remarkable how much direct information dreams can give us.

Another woman who has been working on her relationship with her partner dreams that she is looking into the bathroom mirror and she realizes that she is wearing a "smiling mask." She begins to remove it and it comes off her face like putty as her real face begins to emerge. She was starting to become aware of how much she lived her life pleasing her husband and children and everyone else around her and how much resentment she felt underneath this behavior. The dream showed her the mask she had been wearing, a behavior that was not her but rather a self in her that had taken over when she was very young. Only after becoming aware of the mask does her real face begin to appear.

Chapter 10 will help you understand the language of dreams, give you a sense of the simplicity of many of your dreams, and help you understand certain basic principles of dream work. It is a world of magic unto itself.

Including Spirit in Your Partnering

In every partnering relationship there is a third entity, which is beautifully described in a recent book by Jack Zimmerman, Ph.D., and Jaquelyn McCandless, M.D., entitled *Flesh and Spirit.* The idea of "the third" is simply an acknowledgment of divinity, of the reality of spirit. It is often most clearly seen in the dream process where the intelligence of the unconscious expresses itself quite regularly. Spirit may be experienced in meditation, in extended physical activity, in sexuality, in loving someone or something, or in the use of the mind under certain circumstances. Surrendering to the process of relationship also involves surrendering to the reality of spirit and a willingness to be open to its guidance.

Along with the surrender to this spiritual dimension, there is also the development of individual rituals in partnering that allow us to create ways of honoring the reality of spirit. The development of such rituals has been a very significant part of our lives and we are pleased to share some of this with you.

These are some of the basic considerations that we feel are essential to a partnering relationship. No matter where you are in the relationship process we feel that if you can begin to integrate and implement these principles of partnering, then the quality of all of your relationships will dramatically change. The process of relationship in general and partnering in particular is always a "work in progress." When relationship works, life feels wonderful. When relationship doesn't work, life can feel quite miserable. Is there anything more important in our world today than working on ourselves and our relationships so that we can bring the gifts of partnering to a new generation of children and bring to our own lives a sense of richness and joy that comes with conscious relationship?

In the next chapter we begin our relational journey by entering into the world of the selves and learning the ways in which these selves determine how we function in relationship.

Chapter 2

BUT I THOUGHT I WAS MARRIED TO JUST ONE PERSON! OUR "SELVES" IN RELATIONSHIP

To rediscover the magic of the early days of relationship, to meet again the partner that you once loved so dearly, you must begin a new kind of exploration. This exploration leads to the discovery of the many selves that live within you. These selves interact with your partner's selves and cause all kinds of mischief. As you begin to understand these selves and how they interact, much of the confusion and difficulty of your relationship will become crystal clear.

Relationships are alive. They change; they grow. One of the important lessons we've learned over the years is that whenever we stopped our own growth and tried to keep our patterns of partnering safely static, our relationship died a little.

We discovered that relationships are like plants that require larger containers as they mature. If you try to keep them in the pots that were fine when they were young, they will either die from lack of nourishment or they will continue to grow and eventually burst the vessel that has held them. Over the years, we have seen both. We have seen the pain of long-dead relationships that continue in form but not in feeling and we have seen the anguish of broken committed relationships.

We have been privileged to look at many thousands of relationships. We saw that what worked for people at age seventeen was not necessarily what worked at thirty, or forty when they were trying to balance love, careers, and children. We noticed that life, and relationships, had a tendency to get more complex as people got older. New stages in life made new demands upon partnering.

Happily, we discovered that it was not necessary to lose the passion of the early stages of our relationship, but we did find that the business of life demanded new information, new ways of being in the world, and new ways of relating to one another. It was a challenge.

When we talk about changes and growth, does this mean that you (or we) have been doing things wrong up until now? No, not at all! It just means that there is a possibility to build upon what you *already* have and to move toward a richer, more rewarding relationship.

People seem to expect that everyone instinctively knows all about relationship, that this is part of our original equipment at birth. But that is just not the way it is. There are certain things we know and certain things we do not know. What we do not know, we must learn. This learning is a lifelong process; one that pays great dividends. We think it is fascinating.

Are you wondering where to look for this information? Just look around you; there are an amazing variety of places to go to learn about relating and there is a wealth of information available. Books, magazines, films, even music and art teach us about relationship. You can learn from your therapists and your teachers. There are workshops that train people in relationship skills. You can learn from your family and friends. But most of all, you can learn about partnering from the partnering process itself! So, know that there will always be opportunities for you to learn about the process of relating and to use this learning to understand and improve your partnering.

We have a particular view of partnering and of the lessons to be learned from it. It is based upon a picture of the psyche that we call "the psychology of the aware ego and the selves." Since it is this viewpoint that provides the foundation for this book, we'll spend some time looking at the selves that exist in relationship. (For more detail, read our book *Embracing Our Selves*.)

THE MANY "SELVES" IN RELATIONSHIP

You are not a single entity and neither are we. Each of us is made up of many "selves." These selves are the building blocks of the psyche. They are independent units or personalities. Each of these selves is like an *actual* person living inside of us. Each has its own history, its own way of looking at life, and each has its own way of living in the world. How you will behave in any particular situation will depend upon the self that is in charge at that moment. This is normal; there is nothing strange about it. Let's see what this looks like.

Do you have days (or even moments) at work or at home when you know that you are in charge, when things seem to flow smoothly and the right answers are there when you need them? Then there are the other times when you feel awkward and everything seems wrong. It is as though somebody else inside of you is running the show. Decisions are difficult to make, you have an insecure feeling, you question everything you do, and nothing feels exactly right. Actually, somebody else *is* running the show. There are two different selves operating at these two different times. The first is someone who is both in charge and decisive. The other is an inner critic who criticizes everything you do or say and makes you awkward and insecure.

Here is another example of two different selves as they operate in two different parts of someone's life. Let's look at Helen to see what can happen. Helen is an intelligent, attractive, chic, thirty-five-year-old divorce lawyer who specializes in mediation. She is an uncomplaining, independent person who worked hard to get to this point in her life. It took a lot of discipline to finish college and law school and to pass all her examinations, but Helen persisted and is now a partner in a highly respected law firm. Despite her professional success, her career is not all that is important to her. Helen loves her partner deeply and is devoted to her family and friends. She tries her best to balance both worlds.

Helen is literally one person at work and a different person at home because different selves operate in each of these settings. If you saw Helen at work, you would be impressed with her objectivity and her amazing ability to deal with complex situations and angry clients. She coolly considers the input or needs of others, but she keeps her eye on the objective facts of any situation and deals with it accordingly. When Helen is at work she is totally sure of herself and her ability to see facts clearly and to make the right decisions. Her own emotions and the feelings of others do not affect her in any way. However, when Helen gets home, things are different. She becomes more personal and emotional, more easily influenced by the feelings and needs of the people around her. She cares very much about the feelings and reactions of her partner, her family, and her friends. She wants everybody to love her. At home, Helen's decision making and her actions are deeply affected by the people she loves and the objectivity and coolness that we observe at work is nowhere to be found. Again, these are two different selves. They are operating in two different situations. The first self is one we would call an "objective or impersonal self" and the second is a "personal or feeling self."

What might two different selves look like in a single relationship and a single location? Let's look at Angela who, although also thirty-five years of age, attractive, and quite intelligent, is quite different from Helen. In contrast to Helen, Angela left school after finishing two years of college in order to get married and have children. She loves being at home. She plans to move into the workforce later in life but for now, her husband earns enough money for the family to live comfortably and a career does not look appealing to her. Her mother was not a motherly nurturing type, but a successful saleswoman who had to spend a great deal of time traveling. Angela had been left home with a nanny much of the week when she was young, so she vowed she would put her home and family first when she grew up. She loved playing with dolls and she began to baby-sit for the younger children in the neighborhood when she was quite young. People often commented upon her motherly qualities and her competence with youngsters.

At Thanksgiving Angela spends hours creating a wonderful feast for everyone. She sings as she cooks and truly enjoys the entire day of preparation. She feels creative, full of life and energy. Then, after the meal is over, quite suddenly and without warning, she becomes angry and resentful. She feels exhausted, unappreciated, and generally irritable. She muses to herself that her guests are truly inconsiderate, that nobody else ever does anything to help her, and that everyone always takes advantage of her.

Does this mean that Angela was basically begrudging? That underneath it all she feels like a martyr? No, not at all! These are just two different selves, each doing what it does and, we might add, doing it rather well. The first self is someone who loves to take care of others. This nurturer truly enjoys preparing meals and does not begrudge the time or energy this costs. In contrast, the second self is not a nurturer and sees no value in caring for others. In fact, to this self, the preparation of a meal for others is a waste of time. It is more self-involved; it is a judgmental self that is harshly critical of others and sees all their selfishness and imperfections.

Here, as with Helen, we have two very different selves that operate independently of one another, but in contrast to Helen where her different selves are in different settings, both of Angela's selves operate with her family. You can see how her family is not relating to Angela as a single entity, but to Angela's different selves. This is very confusing for them. They don't know what to think. Is Angela happy to cook Thanksgiving dinner or is she resentful? Remember please, this is just normal relating. There is nothing strange about it.

So, when you are in a relationship this relationship is not between two people but between two groups of selves that are constantly interacting. In Angela's example when you come in contact with her you are relating either to her "nurturing self" or her "judgmental self." You can never be quite sure which one will be in charge at any given moment. This is quite a challenge! (It can also be very exciting because who can be bored when there is so much going on all the time?)

Think about it. Think about how different it is to relate to someone as the selves in charge begin to shift. These selves can be protective or attacking, responsible or irresponsible, nurturing or needy, selflessly giving or selfishly greedy, controlling or passive, dependent or independent, self-assured or self-critical, supportive or judgmental, hovering or unavailable, loving or hateful. There are all kinds of possibilities and they are all in each of us! Even when one of these selves (for instance, the supportive self) is in charge of your partner's life, you may sense the opposite (for instance, the judgmental self) without your partner even being aware of its existence.

When we know about these different selves, much about our relationships becomes clear. When we do not, we are easily hurt, confused, and angered by our partners. We often feel betrayed by them. We bemoan their lack of consistency and question both their truthfulness and their underlying motivations. We ask ourselves questions like: "What ever happened to the wonderful person I married?" "Where did our sexual relationship go?" "Why did he take time out to help us last week if he resented it all along?" "Why doesn't he ever take the time to sit quietly with me these days when he used to say how much he loved doing this in the past?" "Was she hiding her real self from me all along?"

When we do not know about the different selves, we judge our partners with comments like: "All men (or women) are like that underneath!" "You can never trust anyone, they all have hidden agendas." "He (or she) only gives to me with strings attached." We overgeneralize. Or we become critical of our partner and openly criticize him or her. Or perhaps we become withdrawn or depressed. Sometimes we even become critical of ourselves and worry about why we ruin all our relationships. What is the secret of relating that we don't know? Why do others seem to have such smooth, uncomplicated relationships? What did we do that turned this marvelous person into a monster? Some people get so hopeless about relationships that they decide it just is not worth the bother. They're better off alone. Well, we are two people who think it is definitely worth the bother and we would like to make things a bit easier by helping you to begin to recognize the selves and to learn about what really goes on in your relationships.

When you know about the many selves within each of us, changes and inconsistencies are no longer a mystery and you begin to recognize that your partner has not changed at all. It is, instead, the self or selves in charge of your partner's interaction that have changed.

HOW DID WE FIND OUT ABOUT THESE SELVES?

We discovered the existence of these selves in the early 1970s. We had been involved in a mutual exploration with an emphasis on dreams and active imagination. Then something amazing happened. I (Sidra) will never forget the day that Hal asked if he could speak with the little girl in me. At that time, the very last thing I could have ever imagined was that I had a "little girl" in me. If, by any chance, I did have one, it was even more unlikely that she would be sensitive or vulnerable. I smile now as I remember how much I prided myself on being a strong, reasonable, mature woman who did not let her feelings run her life, mess up her relationships, or stand in the way of accomplishing her goals. In those days, I would have been horrified if anyone had ever told me that I was sensitive. I equated sensitivity with irrationality and weakness. After all, I was from New York.

But I did trust Hal and this psycho-spiritual exploration had been fascinating thus far. So I sat on the floor by a coffee table and I rested my head upon it and I tried to let myself become a little girl. It worked! Much to my surprise, I could feel myself change. I could feel the world change. I felt very small, the room became large, and my perceptions became extremely acute. I was suddenly filled with feelings and memories, and I did not want to (and could not) talk. I felt like a little girl who had been safely hiding in a cave for her entire life. I did not want Hal to talk very much. I just wanted him to be there with me. He stayed with me, making occasional comments as I sat there, mostly silent, with pictures flashing through my mind. I felt as I had when I was a very, very little girl. It was astonishing.

When I returned to my chair, I felt like my old (sensible) self again — but with a difference — I knew that this little girl was real and there was no questioning that fact. I knew that there was a lot more to me than the reasonable, mature woman I thought I was.

We both knew that something very important had just happened. We realized that selves did exist. They were not just theoretical constructs. They were not just "complexes" or "patterns of behavior." They were like real people living within us. We then moved on to meet Hal's little boy and from there to meet and talk with many of our other selves. This method of communicating with the selves is what ultimately became known as *voice dialogue*. It was a marvelous period of joint exploration as we came to know each other at deeper and deeper levels and as we learned about the many selves.

Primary Selves

We divided these selves into primary selves and disowned selves. As you can see, Sidra's primary self at that time was a very reasonable and very sensible and rather proper New Yorker. Up until she met this little girl, she had (proudly) disowned all of her more sensitive selves. Hal's primary way of relating in the world was through his wise and very responsible father self. He had (proudly) disowned all his more irresponsible or foolish selves.

This is a very important differentiation because our primary selves and our disowned selves have a great impact on all relationships. In fact, the interplay of these primary and disowned selves between people is responsible for much of the pain and misunderstandings in relationships. What, then, do we mean when we talk about these selves?

Primary selves are the selves that have developed to protect us in the world. They are the basis of our "personalities," our way of being in the world. They are, literally, who we think we are. Basically, it is their job to guard our natural sensitivity and vulnerability and to protect us from pain and failure. They try to earn us love, and they do their best to help us function successfully in our world.

Different primary selves develop in different people. Your primary selves developed to deal with your own life. There is always a good reason why your primary selves are what they are! They have done the best that they could do in light of the specific circumstances of your life. Your own particular group of primary selves was influenced by your genetic coding, your family, the people in your life, your birth order, your culture, your religion, the schools you attended, and the historical period in which you were raised. For those who think in terms of astrology or karma, these too could influence the development of your primary selves.

The key here is that your primary selves are who you think you are. For instance, Bob sees himself as a sensible, rational, responsible person. Bob is a fifty-eight-year-old accountant who has been married to Nancy, his high school sweetheart, for the past thirty-three years and is the father of two successful grown sons. Bob does everything in moderation and with a great deal of planning. His entire retirement is already worked out and his pension is adequately funded. Bob does not talk very much and he is always even tempered. He thinks carefully before he speaks and he has never been known to raise his voice. Bob is proud of the fact that he is not foolish and not easily swayed by his feelings. He knows how to think things through when he makes decisions. Bob learned early in life that emotions are notoriously unpredictable and can be dangerous. His parents were both emotional and irresponsible. Their raging arguments and the unpredictability of their moods frightened Bob and made him feel unsafe. So he developed primary selves that made him feel safe. His primary selves are his "responsible self" and his "rational (or sensible) self."

Primary selves usually emerge early in life, although not always. Bob's primary selves developed very early in life. He began to "figure things out" when he was very young. But *your* primary selves may have developed later. Early in life one of your primary selves may have been a dreamer and you may have enjoyed happy hours alone playing by yourself or daydreaming, but once you went to school this no longer worked. So you developed a new primary self, an achiever, and you put the dreamer away.

Your primary selves *can* change over time, like changing from a dreamer to an achiever — or perhaps from a "good girl" to a "rebel," or from dependent to independent. Sometimes your primary selves change back and forth. You might move from "good girl" to "rebel" and back again to "good girl."

There is another interesting aspect of our primary selves that often has a significant impact on our relationships. *Many of us have different primary selves that operate in different areas of our lives.* You may be a cool, clear businesswoman at work, but turn into a needy incompetent child when you are with your husband. Conversely, your husband may be a responsible, helpful, adult type of person when he is with the neighbors, but when he is at home he seems to become a stubborn child. He has the time and energy to help the man next door repair his entire roof, but he cannot find five minutes to change the washer in your dripping kitchen faucet.

Here we have different primary selves in different situations.

As you might well imagine, these changes can be confusing and irritating. "Why," you might think, "can't my husband find the time to change the faucet?" Or, conversely, he might wonder to himself why you cannot figure out how to balance the checkbook at home when you do such a great job of it at the office. The simple answer is: although it is the same body, you are dealing with different selves.

These different primary selves literally take over in these different situations. It is not a matter of choice because there is no choice. The takeover is automatic. First one primary self drives our psychological car and then, in another situation, another takes over. The changes in behavior are perfectly understandable once we know about the selves and how they operate.

Disowned Selves

Let's return to Bob who, early in life, became very reasonable and kept everything under control. What happened to his emotions? What happened to his natural instinctual energies or his impulses? He got rid of them. They were too dangerous.

Equal and opposite to the primary selves that dominate our lives are the selves that we discard or disown. Bob, in his growing up years, disowned his emotions and his natural instincts. These were not safe. These were the primary selves of his parents and Bob did not want to grow up to be like his parents.

Whatever parts of us we try to get rid of in our personality, life will bring to us in the form of people who are exactly like our disowned selves. We can definitely predict that Bob will meet people who carry his disowned selves. Each time he does, these people will be a challenge for him. He will either be strongly attracted or strongly repelled or some combination of the two. He is very likely to marry an emotional woman. If his wife is not emotional, his oldest child will be emotional, or he will have a very nervous dog. If this does not happen at home, there will be someone at work who lives life in a very emotional way. *Hal has always said that these disowned selves are like heat-seeking missiles, aimed at us by the intelligence of the universe, and find us they will.* There is no escaping them. There is just the challenge to learn our lesson, and to integrate them in a way that is safe and protective.

HOW CAN I DISCOVER MY PRIMARY AND DISOWNED SELVES?

It is surprisingly simple to discover your primary and disowned selves. Your disowned selves are reflected in the qualities that you either judge or overvalue in others. Sometimes you may both overvalue and judge them at the same time. So, when you come across somebody who really pushes your buttons, you can be sure that you have met a person who is carrying your disowned self. Once you determine exactly what it is that you judge about that person, you have discovered one of your own disowned selves. Then, just look for the opposite and you will find your own primary self.

Now let's see how this works. We are going to take you through a very simple exercise. But first, some guidelines. Give yourself uninterrupted time to do the exercises in this book so that you can give adequate thought to your answers. Even ten or fifteen minutes will do. Relax and center yourself by taking a few deep breaths before you start. Write down your thoughts as they occur, do not censor them. There are no right answers. It is often helpful to keep these exercises in one place like a notebook, a file folder, or a new folder in your computer. You might even want to start a journal devoted to the relationships in your life and include these exercises, additional thoughts you might have about your present or past relationships, and any dreams that you might have as you read this book and think about your relationships. Keep this material in a private place so that you can be totally free in your thoughts and your writing.

DISOWNED SELF EXERCISE 1
Judging Your Disowned Self

Think of someone in your life who pushes your buttons — perhaps a family member, a current partner, or a partner from the past — somebody you judge. (This should not require a great deal of thought. Pick a person who really annoys you, hopefully someone who has annoyed you for years.) What is it about that person that you judge? In which area do you feel superior? Be specific as you write down the most irritating or reprehensible attribute of this person. When you discover what this is, you have learned about one of your own disowned selves. Whatever it is that you judge about this person is one of your disowned selves.

Now look for the opposite quality in yourself and see how you contrast with this person. What kind of person are you? What are the qualities that you are proud of having? Write down these qualities. You have just described one of your primary selves.

You now have a picture of one of your primary selves and one of your disowned selves.

(You can repeat this exercise as many times as you wish to discover more of your primary and disowned selves.)

Let's say that for this exercise you have chosen your partner as the person you judge. What is it you judge? Perhaps you think that your partner is too selfish, too self-involved. You, in contrast, are usually available to others when they need you and you feel that caring for others and being considerate of their needs is a very important part of life.

We would say that your primary self requires you to act in a responsible way and that you disown your own selfish or self-nurturing self. This primary self, this caretaker, has very strong negative reactions to people who are not caretakers. It is this primary self that judges your partner and finds his or her behavior reprehensible.

This is a common set of opposites that we find in relationship.

One partner gives other people's needs first priority and the other partner takes care of his or her needs first. Which one is right? Neither is right. No self is completely good and no self is completely bad. Each has something to contribute to the system and each person in the relationship has something important to teach the other. What is important is that we develop an ability to stand between these opposites and learn how to use them both in a new way.

Taking care of others is neither good nor bad, it is simply taking care of others. Being tuned into one's own needs and taking care of oneself is neither good nor bad, it is simply having the ability to take care of oneself.

DISOWNED SELF EXERCISE 2
Overvaluing the Other Person

Now think of someone you overvalue, someone you yearn for, someone who is so wonderful that you feel decidedly "less than" when that person is around. This person also carries one of your disowned selves. Again, be specific about what it is about this person that is so wonderful. For instance, you may have chosen a former lover who is very well organized and always seems calm, cool, and collected. Once you have figured this out, write down a description of this quality. You have found another disowned self, your "organized, calm, cool, and collected" self.

To discover your primary self, look for the opposite in yourself. What kind of person are you? As you think about it, you, in contrast to this former lover, are disorganized and always a bit frazzled. You have found a primary self, it is disorganized and a bit frazzled.

These disowned selves that we overvalue are often our fatal attractions, the people we feel that we cannot live without. How does this work? In very practical terms, we become attached to people who fill in our missing pieces, people who carry our disowned selves. For example, you might be the kind of person who does what is expected and follows the rules. You are cautious and think always of how others will react to what you do or say. We would say that your primary self is a strict rule-maker who wants to be sure that you always do the right thing; it is a self that is always concerned with what people will think about your behavior.

Because of this, you admire the self-confident people of the world, the free spirits who do not worry about what others think. The partner you choose is like this. She never worries about what others think. She lives her own life and does as she pleases. She is not foolish or antisocial, she is just very independent. When you are with her, you feel safe. She is able to reassure you; she helps you to be more independent of the opinions of others and she encourages you not to worry so much about the rules. She is your "fatal attraction": you feel as though you need her desperately and that your life is incomplete when she is not around.

Which kind of person should you be, one who follows rules or one who does not worry about them? Which of these is right? Again, neither is right. Each of you has something to learn from the other.

THE BASIC LAW OF RELATIONSHIP: LEARNING TO WORK WITH OUR SELVES

Whatever we disown is what we attract. This is the basic law of relationship. It is almost as though there is a kind of intelligence within us that moves us in a particular direction. Some refer to it as "entelechy," the purposive nature of the psyche that pushes us to complete ourselves, to become all that we can become. It senses what we are missing and then pushes (or pulls) us to fill the vacuum. Of course, what we are missing is what we have disowned. *If we think of relationship as the vehicle for completing ourselves, then we see each of the people who carry our disowned selves as our teachers.*

It was fascinating — as well as challenging and often difficult — for us to learn from one another in this way. We carried so many of each other's disowned selves, we sometimes wondered whether our relationship would survive. Hal was a spiritual intuitive and Sidra was a rational pragmatist. Hal was interested in the process and Sidra was interested in the solution. Hal was a laid-back Californian and Sidra was a proper New Yorker. Hal was UCLA and Sidra was Barnard. Hal was a spender and Sidra was a saver. Hal was dedicated to his mission on earth and Sidra was dedicated to her children. Hal was an introvert and Sidra was an extrovert. This list may not be endless, but it certainly covers a vast territory.

Over the years, we sometimes overvalued the disowned selves that we carried for one another but, more often, we judged them and tried to change them. Until we became aware of this basic law of the psyche, we usually saw these disowned selves as the enemy and there were times they caused us much pain. A great deal of the pain that people experience in relationship is based on the fact that they have no understanding that they are carrying each other's disowned selves.

This is true in all relationships. At first, we may find our disowned selves irresistible when we see them in our partner, and then we usually find them impossible. Sometimes we find them both irresistible and impossible at the same time. Very confusing, very upsetting, isn't it? But that is just the way things are. We believe we have discovered an explanation for all of this that we present as a fantasy called the "great computer in the sky."

Our fantasy is that the intelligence of the universe has representatives in heaven whose job it is to help each of us embrace all the different parts of ourselves so that we can become fully who and what we were meant to be. These people have a large computer in the sky which is programmed with information about all the people in the world. This database has a very special category — a listing of each person's primary and disowned selves. When the representatives decide to evaluate someone they look at the primary selves of the person and then figure out who they need to be with in order to meet their disowned selves.

For instance, when they were examining Hal they found that he was very mental, very responsible, very spiritual, and not too grounded so far as business and finance were concerned. His journeys were all on the inside and the world felt very unsafe to him. So they started their computer going. Around and around it buzzed and then it landed on Sidra. Hal will love her so that will balance his mind. She loves to travel, so she will introduce him to the wonders of the world outside of California. Since she has a strong need for financial security, she'll teach him about money and savings and how to plan for the future. Of course, he will teach her about the things he knows. He will introduce her to the world of the spirit and to the meaning of her dreams. He will teach her about honoring the process as an alternative to rushing toward solution. They will either kill each other with their judgments or they will recognize the higher meaning of all relationships, their own included. And what is this higher meaning? It is to understand that all relationship, when understood and used properly, can become our teacher, healer, and guide.

YOUR PARTNER IS YOUR TEACHER

The people in our lives who carry our disowned selves are our teachers. When we realize this, life and relationships look different. This is true of everybody in our lives, not only our partners; but it is usually our primary relationship that carries the biggest charge. Let's take a look at how this works, using one of our own sets of disowned selves that the great computer noted in the last section.

It was early in our marriage and Hal had a number of debts he wanted settled. Hal had generously supported the Center for the Healing Arts for many years because he felt strongly that the introduction of a holistic approach to healing was truly important. He had borrowed money in order to do this. In contrast, Sidra had been extremely conservative throughout the years in her spending, never buying on credit (not even a car). She always lived well within her income, and she had a substantial equity in her home.

One evening, at dinner, Hal suggested that Sidra refinance her home in order to pay off his debts. With the freedom of speech that came after two martinis, Sidra (who is usually more tactful) said: "I would never do anything like that! Giving you money would be like pissing it down the drain," and she laughed. This is what a primary self sounds like when it is threatened. Sidra's "thrifty housefrau," horrified by Hal's "spender," could never part with that money, even if it would cost Sidra the relationship.

At that point we had a choice. We could have become enemies. If we had, Hal would have seen Sidra as an inconsiderate, selfish miser and Sidra would have seen Hal as an undisciplined profligate spender. Each of us could have enlisted sympathetic supporters from among our friends and families who would agree that the other person was simply impossible. The war could have escalated.

Instead, we realized that there was a lesson in this for each of us. Hal immediately saw his lesson and began to watch the way he handled his finances. He used Sidra as a teacher. He never lost his basic generosity with money, but he now thought first before he committed funds anywhere. Conversely, Sidra began to lighten up a bit. We used to joke about the tiny little purse she would grudgingly open in order to hand out a few pennies. Without losing contact with her primary self — we called her the thrifty housefrau — Sidra learned to spend money not only for the basic necessities but for pure enjoyment as well. She integrated Hal's generosity and ease, and life was a lot more fun.

Each of us learned to stand between the opposites — we could feel the self that wanted us to spend and, at the same time, we could feel the self that wanted us to save. This is a pretty straightforward example from our own experience and it gives the basic paradigm for learning the lessons that life is able to teach us through our relationships.

These apparently irreconcilable differences in relationships, the places where we bump up against our own disowned selves as they are mirrored back to us by our partners, are opportunities for the greatest growth. Our primary selves do not like what they see in the mirror, but as we separate from these primary selves and make use of this larger perspective, there is another world waiting for us. We begin to see the value of the selves carried by our partners. We get a sense of what it is that we are missing and we have the chance to claim this for ourselves.

As we reclaim these disowned selves — without losing our primary selves — we usually reclaim our relationship. The partner who looked so impossible (e.g., too frugal or too irresponsible) a moment ago suddenly looks just fine again and you're glad that he (or she) is still around.

HOW CAN I LEARN THE LESSONS THAT RELATIONSHIP HAS TO TEACH ME?

All this may sound daunting, but it really is not. The first thing to do is to start to think about yourself and your relationships in a new way. *Think in terms of the many selves — both yours and your partner's — and watch how these selves behave. If you do no more than this, you will have accomplished a great deal; you will have changed the way you approach relationship. You will be living relationship as a joint venture.*

For instance, your partner is particularly irritating today. Last night when you were relaxing together, you liked him a lot, but now he infuriates you as he slowly sips his coffee. He seems to be accomplishing absolutely nothing while you have a million important things to do and there is not enough time to take care of them all. You look at your calendar book and it is crammed full of appointments and lists. You look at your partner with silent fury and wish he would get moving.

You have two choices here. You can work harder and harder and get more and more angry as you watch your partner enjoy himself, or you can step back and say to yourself: "Could this be what I was just reading about? I am judging him and I feel a great deal of anger. Could I be looking at my disowned self? Is there a lesson for me here?"

We would encourage you to make the latter choice. After all, why be miserable? Why throw out a perfectly good partner because he knows how to enjoy a good cup of coffee in the morning? Besides, wouldn't it be nice if you knew how to slow down?

If your partner is carrying your disowned self— and we assure you that he is — then you have a clue about which self is in charge of your life. It is a self we call "the pusher." The pusher is a very popular primary self, especially among successful people. The pusher knows how to fill in appointment books, make lists, and get things done. As a matter of fact, that is all the pusher knows. But he does his job well. The problem is that your pusher does not have a turn-off switch. He can only move in one direction; he can only speed up. In contrast, your partner has a primary self that is more relaxed. His primary self has as its main rule in life: "Enjoy yourself, it's later than you think."

As you figure out the lesson in this, you have already accomplished a great deal. You have gotten a picture of your own inner pusher (usually a much more demanding taskmaster than the outer pushers of the world) and you have separated from it. This immediately makes life look more manageable and you will feel far less harassed and irritable.

You now have some choice in your behavior. You might even be able to join your partner for a relaxing cup of coffee before you begin your day. This would mean that you have actually separated from your primary self (the pusher) and begun to integrate the more relaxed self that your partner carries. It would mean that when you do begin your day, it will be *you* and not your pusher who does the work.

What a difference this makes! As you separate from your primary self (the pusher) you no longer look at the world through its eyes. Life is no longer a series of pressing chores and obligations. Your partner no longer irritates you as he had a moment ago, when your pusher was evaluating his behavior. As a matter of fact, your partner who just a moment ago was looking like the laziest man on

Earth is beginning to look like a human being again — and an attractive one at that.

You have just seen how we can use our judgments of our partners and, conversely, their judgments of us, as clues that point us toward the discovery of our disowned selves, the missing parts of our personality. *What we judge in others are our disowned selves. When we realize this we can spare ourselves — and our partners — a great deal of pain.* Unfortunately (for those of us who like to feel superior) we also lose that great feeling of self-righteous moral superiority.

We do not want to underestimate the discomfort these judgments can create. Our judgments of our partners, and their judgments of us, are usually pretty unpleasant. Sometimes they are more than unpleasant; sometimes they can be downright miserable and hurt dreadfully. On a really bad day, they can damage a relationship beyond repair.

However, these judgments are gold mines of information. When your partner looks lazy to you and you are feeling extremely irritable, you can be sure that you are in the grips of your pusher. When your partner seems too uncaring, you are probably in the grips of your caretaker and it is likely that you have become excessively caring. In the same vein, your partner's judgments of you carry a lesson and a message. When you are in the grips of your caretaker, your partner will judge you for giving away too much of your time. When your pusher is in charge, your partner will complain that you are a workaholic or that you are too driven.

STANDING ON ONE FOOT IS UNSTABLE — INTRODUCING THE AWARE EGO

When you live your life through a primary self it is as though you are hopping through life on only one leg — without a crutch. Picture what this is like. You are unstable and easily pushed over. This makes relationships difficult. If you are able to stand between opposites — that is, between two opposing selves like the spender and the saver — you have two legs to stand on and it is not so easy to push you over. Let's see how this works.

Bernie is responsible, careful, thoughtful, and really nice, and the oldest of three children. He's also very handsome and smart and plays a great game of soccer, but that has nothing much to do with his primary selves. Although Bernie is only twenty-nine years old, he is already respected by his colleagues and has been offered a partnership in his accounting firm. Everybody seems to lean on him, even his parents. Bernie is a handy guy. He can repair just about anything around the house and it seems as though he knows just about everything there is to know about computers as well.

Bernie is married to Annie, a perfectly delightful twenty-five-year-old. She works as an artist illustrating children's books. Annie is an only child, and her parents absolutely doted on her when she was growing up. They encouraged her to express herself in every aspect of life and did everything they could to enhance her creativity. They made few demands on her and were only too happy to take responsibility for the less exciting aspects of life. So Annie does not think very much about responsibility, finances, or the future. Instead, she is creative, spontaneous, and is often a lot of fun. Since she does not worry very much about the consequences of her actions, she often takes risks. Annie's primary self is a charming free spirit who doesn't worry about the future and is not particularly concerned with the needs or expectations of others.

In contrast, Bernie's primary self is very responsible and very nice. If somebody needs something from him, he must be responsive to this need. He is always available, giving advice, time, and even money when it is needed. He is the proverbial rock that everybody leans upon. Even though Bernie looks strong and solid, he is going through life on only one leg — the leg of the responsible father — and, because of this, he is basically unstable. If his wife, Annie, wants to destabilize him, she has only to accuse him of being selfish. She may say: "You never think of others, but only of yourself." He is very upset by this because according to the rules of his primary self he must responsibly take care of everyone's needs — including those of his family — which he feels he does pretty well.

Bernie would be no more stable if he were to adopt a more selfish and self-serving philosophy of life. This often happens as people go into rebellion against their original way of being. He would be merely trading one leg for the other. Instead of Mr. Nice Guy being available, his new primary self would be Mr. Selfish who always puts himself first and automatically says no to others.

If Bernie were not living life either as a responsible father or as a more selfish person, he would be standing between these opposites. He would be able to make a choice when someone needed him. He would be able to embrace the good father in him with one arm and his more selfish side with his other arm. He would begin to have a choice about how much to give or not give. He would be standing on both legs embracing these two important opposites.

Now exactly *who* is the Bernie who is able to do this? It is not the same Bernie who was always responsible. That Bernie was identified with his primary self and his primary self *automatically* made all his decisions. The new Bernie is operating from what we call the *aware ego*. It is this aware ego that learns how to stand between opposites. By developing an aware ego, Bernie can stand between his responsible nature and his selfish nature and have some real choice in deciding what works for him and what does not work for him. (For more information on the aware ego, see the list of books and tapes at the end of this book.)

This aware ego is very important. When you operate from an aware ego, you have separated from a primary self and have broadened your options by gaining access to the selves that you have disowned. You are no longer dominated by the rules and requirements of your primary self, but you still have access to its ideas and opinions. This gives you much new information and the freedom to make healthier, more creative decisions. You, like Bernie, will be able to make real choices and you will be less easily destabilized by either judgment or self-criticism. All this adds up to a totally new way of relating to others.

There is no free will until you develop an aware ego process that can stand between opposites. We call it a "process" because the aware ego is not static but is constantly evolving and changing over time. Only then is it possible to make real choices, whatever the opposites may be. Now that Bernie stands firmly on two legs between opposites, he can either give or not give, depending upon the situation. As a responsible father, he must give no matter what the consequence to his emotional, physical, or financial well-being. From his more self-serving nature, he would be impervious to the needs of others and feel only his own needs. Each contributes its piece of information to Bernie, who can then process it and make a choice about what he will do.

It is difficult for our "two-legged" Bernie operating from an aware ego to be destabilized by Annie's judgment. Now when she says to him: "You never think of others, but only of yourself," he realizes that this is not true. Indeed, sometimes he does put his own needs first, as in this particular situation, but at other times he puts others' needs first. It all depends on the situation. He can listen to her comment and it will not automatically destabilize him because he has no rigid rule demanding one kind of behavior or the other. There is no destabilization and no reason to become upset. A major argument has been avoided. There is a deep change in the nature of their relationship and an increased stability and trust.

Understanding How Destabilization Can Undermine Your Relationship

When you are standing only on the foot of your primary self, you are easily destabilized. If you lose your equilibrium — and, we might add, your sense of humor — you can assume that you have come up against a pair of primary and disowned selves that are operating in your relationship. This does not mean that the relationship is over, it just means there is a clue waiting to be noticed. What might this look like?

Mark and Sandy have been married for fifteen years. They worked hard over the past ten years to build a successful restaurant with Mark as an inspired, creative chef and Sandy as a competent, careful, and charming hostess. Since they have no children, the restaurant is their major creation together. They have done very well as partners at work, but recently they have begun to invest their money in the stock market. Destabilization threatens their relationship because, when it comes to investment strategy, their different primary selves come to the fore.

Sandy is naturally fearful and hates to take risks. Mark, on the other hand, is more impulsive. He makes decisions quickly and is a risk taker. In the development of the restaurant, these two different styles were complementary with Mark pushing for new ideas and Sandy working slowly and methodically to implement them. But the stock market is a different story. Mark has just heard about some great new stock offering and he's ready to move before it's too late to take advantage of this unusual opportunity. Sandy, on the other hand, is afraid of losing their hard-earned money in this investment and wants to take her time and investigate everything thoroughly.

As she gets destabilized, Sandy judges Mark for being too impulsive in his decision making. If Mark becomes destabilized by Sandy's judgment, he can react in one of two ways. He can become angry and judgmental or he can withdraw and feel like a victim. Either one means trouble. Let's assume for a moment that Mark has done his work and that he is aware of the more impulsive side of his nature as well as his more cautious side. He is standing on two legs between opposites and operating from his new aware ego. What happens then? He is not destabilized. He can receive the criticism from Sandy and handle it in a very different way. He has to become neither victim nor attacker. He sees it less as a criticism and more as a comment or observation from Sandy, and so is able to respond to her in a more appropriate and even affirming way.

There is no right or wrong in this situation. Sandy is destabilized and expresses it by judgment. She has to learn to express her fears about risk taking and she also has to learn to embrace Ms. Impulse as well as Ms. Caution in her own personality. Then she doesn't need to judge. Instead, she will be more accepting of Mark's behavior.

Each of the partners is faced with a challenge. Mark is faced with the challenge of separating from his impulsive self and learning how to use caution. Sandy is faced with the challenge of separating from her cautious self and learning about her own impulsive risk taker. They are both using their judgments as a searchlight to discover the work they need to do to complete themselves. They each carry the medicine that the other one needs. *When they approach their differences as a part of a joint venture, this totally changes the nature of their relationship. They move from enemies to partners.* We would consider this a real improvement!

Understanding Polarization

What happens if they do not do this and the destabilization continues? If Mark and Sandy do not view their differences as a challenge and learn from one another, then their primary and disowned selves become increasingly exaggerated as they play out their accustomed roles. As this process continues — and it feels like an out-of-control train running downhill — the partners move into opposing armed camps as they defend their positions and intensify their judgments of one another. We call this *polarization*. As this happens, we see Sandy become more and more cautious and Mark more and more impulsive. Each of them would become more and more judgmental of the other until they can hardly bear to be together.

In primary relationships there are a number of primary and disowned pairings that get intensified by this process of polarization. Perhaps the most common are the ones that John Gray has written about in his book *Men Are from Mars, Women Are from Venus.*

Gray describes several different sets of gender-based primary selves: men's are impersonal, rational, and introverted and women's are personal, feeling, and extroverted. While these differences are to be respected, we feel that each person has a real teaching to offer the other in terms of the disowned selves that his or her primary selves bring out in their partner.

Other differences that have a tendency to become polarized in relationship are: responsible/irresponsible, pusher/relaxed, organized/disorganized, assertive/passive, able to set boundaries/not able to set boundaries, outgoing/withdrawn, spender/saver, worrying about what people will think/not caring, and rule follower/rebel. Any set of opposite selves can polarize in relationship. Let's look at some more examples of this.

Perhaps you have noticed that there are certain people who make you feel responsible for them. The more responsible you are, the less responsible they seem to be. Children are particularly good at doing this. You feel responsible for their homework, their health, and their ability to succeed in the world. The more responsibility you take, the more they give you. The more responsible you are, the less responsible they need to be. Your primary self is "responsible," theirs is "not responsible."

This can also happen at work when there is a job to be done. At one of our workshops we met Edward, an unmarried, hard-working surgeon. Many women had tried to lead him to the altar, but he had never found anyone who was perfect enough. Edward's primary way of handling life was by being compulsively competent and controlling. He felt that the only way to do the work properly was to do it himself; and so this is what he usually did.

Although Edward was a control freak, he needed help to run his office. In a period of six months he had hired and fired six nurses, blaming each one for being impossibly incompetent. Edward's controlling self was in charge of his office and was constantly criticizing the incompetence of the nurses who came to work for him. The more competent and controlling he got, the more incompetent and out of control they became. Their differences became more and more pronounced and polarized.

We see this kind of polarization everywhere, but it is particularly noticeable (and troublesome) in relationships between parents and children. A tidy parent is guaranteed to have at least one untidy child. That child is likely to get more and more untidy in the parental home while the parent becomes ever more distraught. Funnily enough, once that child moves out of the house, it is quite likely that she or he will keep a tidy home because there is no longer anyone to polarize against.

Let's see what this looks like with siblings. We often say that siblings divide up the pie of primary selves. Each takes a particular piece, decides it's the best, and then judges everyone else's piece. For instance, the older brother becomes a high achiever and wins educational honors while the younger brother does poorly at school. The better the first performs, the less well the second does, until it is hard to believe that they are from the same family and have been gifted with a similar intelligence. Two sisters polarize over their looks with the older paying a great deal of attention to her appearance while the younger totally ignores hers. The more fuss the older sister makes, the more the younger sister will judge her for being shallow and the less attention she will give to her own looks.

These polarizations occur in all relationships, both personal and professional, and the judgments that accompany them cause great discomfort and destabilization. However, as we have showed you, there is a great deal that we can learn from our judgments and destabilizations. They are the searchlights that illuminate our disowned selves.

Learning from Self-Criticism

Just as judgment — either our own or our partner's — can destabilize us, so too can self-criticism. When you are identified with a primary self, you are pressured to follow the rules of that primary self. When you fail to follow these rules, your inner critic comes in to enforce them and it attacks you. Once the inner critic gets a foothold, it has a tendency to move into adjacent territory, liberally spreading criticism wherever it goes. It may be some time before you can escape the inner critic's barrage of negative comments about who you are, what you look like, and how you behave.

We can guarantee that once your inner critic has attacked successfully, you will be destabilized. (For more discussion of the inner critic, see our book *Embracing Your Inner Critic*.) One of the best defenses against the attack of the inner critic is the ability to step back from the rules of the primary self and to stand between opposites. What does this look like?

Let's learn from Sally. Sally is a sixty-year-old woman who lives with Anne, her partner of thirty years, their five cats, and a pair of llamas in a beautifully renovated old farmhouse in Vermont. Both Anne and Sally are successful freelance writers. Sally comes from a background that valued perfection and her primary self is, understandably, a perfectionist. (After all, that was Sally's best way to fit in with the family.) Her perfectionist's main rule is "If it's important enough to do, it's important enough to do perfectly." We have no argument with the idea of doing things well. However, it is apparent that a rule like this one is really a setup for self-criticism. After all, who can always be perfect? The inner critic is famous for talking about our "mistakes" and our "failures." With a perfectionist as a primary self, Sally is pressured to behave perfectly in her relationship. She must never do anything that might create problems in the relationship and she must never, ever make a "mistake."

If Sally goes to the store and accidentally picks up a bag of dog food instead of the cat food she meant to buy, she can simply return the dog food to the store and buy the cat food. But when the perfectionist is in charge (with the inner critic following close behind) this becomes a dreadful mistake; Sally is destabilized and thinks to herself: "How could I be so stupid?"

When Sally notices that she is dominated by the perfectionist and separates from its way of thinking, she has some choices in life. With the perfectionist driving her psychological car, Sally has no choice; everything must always be done perfectly and her relationship should always be running smoothly. With Sally in charge there would be priorities. Not everything would have to be perfect. She could buy dog food instead of cat food and it would not become a national catastrophe.

Sally might even move on to the next step, in which she would no longer be under pressure to do anything perfectly. Instead, Sally is permitted to do the best she can and her best is good enough. She might even get in touch with a group of disowned selves that do not care at all about perfection. These selves would rather finish things quickly rather than perfectly. They do not care about what people think, they do not fear criticism, they enjoy leisure, and they love lying in the sun and doing nothing. Sally is now able to walk through life with one arm around her perfectionist and the other arm around her sunbather, a free spirit who does not care one bit about perfection. She has choice about when and where to strive for perfection and life is a great deal more pleasant.

What happens if there is no longer a rule about doing everything perfectly? Sally's inner critic would have far less to criticize!

How does this relate to Sally and her partner? In the past, when Sally's partner criticized her for "making a mistake," she felt terrible because her inner critic agreed with the partner's judgments of her. Together, they accused her of making a mistake. But, when Sally separates from the rule that says she cannot make mistakes, she is no longer destabilized by her partner's judgment. She no longer needs to defend herself, nor does she need to beat herself up "for being so stupid." She can listen to the judgment and consider what her partner is saying, but the emotional charge is missing. Sally's partner is no longer capable of pushing her buttons. Now she can buy canary food instead of cat food and it doesn't matter. It was the rule about being perfect that exposed Sally to the years of destabilization.

You can see from this example exactly how this destabilization in the relationship gave Sally access to a new way of being in the world. The destabilization led Sally to discover the underlying rule she had been living by and, beyond that, it led to the primary self that had made that rule. This enabled her to separate from her perfectionism and to begin to embrace some very new and exciting ways of being in the world.

By now, you have a clear picture of how opposite selves attract — and later repel — one another and how much you can learn from this. Learning about the gifts these disowned selves bring to you and to your relationships changes your partner from a problem to a teacher. It is important to keep in mind that every disowned self becomes one of God's (or the universe's) heat seeking missiles. Once we know this and begin to play with the missiles instead of cursing them, the relationship has a chance to develop into a dance rather than change into the torture chamber it so often becomes. Now let's take the next step and see how these selves interact in our relationships.

Chapter 3

MAPMAKING FOR PARTNERS: UNDERSTANDING THE PATTERNS IN YOUR RELATIONSHIP

It's not what you say, it's who says it.

We made an amazing discovery soon after we were married. We realized that, despite our deep devotion to each other and our years of psychological work, we were slipping into old patterns of behavior that we recognized from our previous marriages. We decided that this simply would not do. We were determined to find out what was going on. We were determined not to diminish the quality of connection we experienced before the marriage.

So we set about looking at our interactions — each and every one of them. We already knew about the many selves. We also knew about primary and disowned selves and the way that they drive each other into greater and greater polarization. Now it was time to look at how the selves interact in relationship.

We realized that we were losing the "us" somehow. We saw that something else had come in and taken over. We also knew that what was happening was perfectly natural. We had seen it in our previous relationships and in the relationships of others.

We wanted to see if there was a repetitive pattern in the apparent chaos and discomfort we were experiencing. As we looked at each painful interaction, a very simple underlying pattern became clear. It was, in fact, so simple that we doubted its universality. But, each time we looked, there it was.

The lessons learned from these "bonding patterns," as we call them, are some of the most important and the most liberating lessons that you will ever learn. They have consistently been among the most important lessons for ourselves and for the many people whose lives we have been privileged to touch. (For a detailed discussion of bonding patterns, see our book *Embracing Each Other.*)

When you learn to recognize your bonding patterns, you gain the ability to separate from them rather than from your partner. As a matter of fact, they provide great fertilizer for your relationship. This means that your bonding patterns can help you grow. When we do not know about our negative bonding patterns, we assume that there is something fatally flawed in (1) our partners, (2) ourselves, (3) all men/all women or, lastly, (4) all relationships.

INTRODUCING BONDING PATTERNS

We named this underlying pattern a *bonding pattern* because it is the term used for the bonding of parent and infant. It is the natural way we humans give and receive nourishment: we bond to one another as parent to child and child to parent. If this bonding does not occur properly in early life, then the infant will not be able to receive adequate nourishment and may well die. That is pretty basic!

Throughout life, people use their bonding patterns to interact with one another when their interactions are governed by their *selves* rather than by their *whole person,* or their *entire self.* If people were computers, we would say that this is the default position of human relations. *There is nothing abnormal about these bonding patterns and we will never be free of them.* But, just as we can learn from the interplay between the primary and disowned selves in relationship, we can learn from what happens in these bonding patterns.

The bonding pattern is the parent-child relationship that develops between two people. Different selves take over the psyche and it is these selves that do the talking. In the following example, the interaction is between the parental side of one person, Annie, and the child self of the second person, Bernie. Simultaneously, there is an interaction between the child self of Annie and the parent self of Bernie. Annie and Bernie essentially disappear. Their lives are now being run by these interacting selves. Let's look at Annie and Bernie's bonding patterns to see how they work.

Annie got a small raise at work because her last set of illustrations had helped boost book sales. On her way home she had time to think about what she would like to do with the money and she began to picture what it would be like to have a new car. By the time she got home, she had already decided on a big beautiful new Jeep Cherokee.

Now, Annie was never great at finances so Bernie had always taken care of figuring out how much money was available for purchases. This time, however, Annie got so excited about her new car that Bernie was literally swept away by her enthusiasm. He lovingly thought of how much she looked like a little girl at Christmastime.

Bernie felt a momentary pang of vulnerability because he was not sure that they had enough money to cover the new vehicle. But he quickly pushed his doubts aside as he generously and lovingly agreed that the Jeep was a wonderful idea. He felt wonderful — a bit like Santa Claus. Annie was delighted and loving. She told him what a wonderful person he was, and they had a delicious night of celebration.

Sometime that night, Bernie woke up feeling anxious. The reality of the finances had come crashing through to him. There was simply not enough money to cover this proposed expense. He felt betrayed by Annie although he could not exactly say why. Then he became irritated with her for being such a demanding, unrealistic woman and he realized that he felt pushed around by her a great deal of the time. Forgetting the lovely evening they had just spent together, he tossed and turned for the remainder of the night.

In the morning Annie woke up to find a cold and distant Bernie. She felt uneasy, betrayed and, for some mysterious reason, a little bit guilty. When she thought about the guilty feeling, she reviewed her actions of the night before and decided that she had not done anything wrong. So, with some irritation, she asked him, "Is anything wrong?" to which he coolly responded, "Nothing. I just have a lot of work to do today." She tried her best to get him to talk to her but nothing worked and Bernie left the apartment as quickly as he could, still thinking about how shabbily he had been treated by Annie. Annie felt abandoned and alone and wondered what had happened. As she reviewed the events of the night before, she became more and more angry with Bernie for behaving unfairly.

As you look at what happened between Annie and Bernie, there is nothing wrong with what they did. It is nobody's fault. These kinds of interactions happen all the time. They are just part of normal living and normal relating. But, if you look for the bonding patterns, you can see that Annie and Bernie got lost and it was their parent and child selves that were interacting. They interact positively in the positive bonding pattern and negatively in the negative bonding pattern.

It was not Bernie who said yes to Annie when she told him about the Jeep. It was a "good father" — a loving and giving self — in Bernie that said yes. Bernie, if he had thought about it at all, would have looked at the financial implications of this decision before he said yes. Good father selves always say yes before considering the practical consequences of their actions. Annie, on the other hand, was not present either. It was her charming daughter — an enthusiastic and seductive self — who originally talked about the new Jeep and effectively seduced Bernie's good father, and it was Annie's approving mother who told Bernie's son how wonderful he was. *This is a positive bonding pattern, not a partnership.*

When Bernie woke up cold and distant in the morning, it was a "bad father" — a judgmental, irritated, and withdrawn self — that had taken over. The judgmental, withdrawn fathers of the world rarely speak out loud; instead they judge silently, making everyone around them miserable. Just as it had not been Bernie who said yes to Annie, now it is not Bernie who is irritably judging her behavior. Annie is not present either. Instead of Annie, we have a defensive daughter who refuses to accept responsibility in this interaction and an angry mother who lets him know how selfish he is. Again we can see the selves taking over the interactions as the default setting of relationship begins to operate. Although, by now, both partners may be wondering whether intimate relating is worth this discomfort, *this is not the end of the relationship, it is only a negative bonding pattern.*

Since this concept of bonding patterns is very important, we will look at these interactions from several angles. First, we will examine positive bonding patterns and negative bonding patterns. See if you can recognize anything familiar in these. For each bonding pattern we will give you a diagram that shows what typically happens between people caught in that pattern and how they feel. Then, we will show you how to map the interaction so that you have an unemotional, objective picture of the bonding pattern.

THE POSITIVE BONDING PATTERN

This interaction between a "loving parent" and a "good child" is what we call a *positive bonding pattern*. The positive bonding pattern is not good — it is neither bad nor good. We call it positive because it feels pretty good to most people and creates a sense of warmth, safety, and predictability that they like. Annie and Bernie's positive bonding pattern feels very comfortable to them. Let's picture this bonding pattern as two photos in one of those double photo frames.

In the left-hand photo we see Bernie, looking very fatherly and loving, sitting in front of a Christmas tree dressed up in a Santa Claus suit. On his lap he holds a darling young version of Annie who smiles up at him adoringly as he gives her a present. To her, he looks like all the good things in the world rolled into one. To him, she is his wonderful little girl. This is a picture of Bernie's "father self" bonding with Annie's "daughter self."

To balance this — and all bonding patterns are perfectly, mathematically balanced — we see another photo in the right-hand half of the frame. It is a picture of Annie's "mother self" bonding with Bernie's "son self." In this picture, Annie is the grown-up loving mother, beaming down at a proud young version of Bernie who is holding a test paper in his hand that has a big A on it. To him, she is all that is loving, encouraging, and accepting. To her, he is her wonderful little man who knows just how to succeed in the world.

These pictures illustrate how Bernie has basically disappeared and been replaced by this very loving and giving "Santa Claus" father. It is a role he knows very well, which is why we call it a *primary self*. This giving father is relating to a part of Annie that can best be described as an enthusiastic, seductive daughter. On the other side of the bonding pattern, Annie has disappeared to be replaced by a very nurturing and approving mother who is interacting with the part of Bernie that is a young achiever who needs approval from his mother.

When this positive bonding pattern is activated by Annie's desire to buy a Jeep, Bernie, as the generous, loving, responsible father, must say yes to Annie's request. Annie's request comes not from the woman, Annie, but from the little girl who wants a new car. Conversely, Annie's approving mother, as she smiles with gratitude and appreciation, makes Bernie's little boy feel just wonderful about himself. Annie and Bernie truly love each other and freely give to each other from these parental selves. There is no holding back. And each inner child feels warm, safe, and loved in the "arms" of the other's inner parent.

Your own positive bonding patterns will look a good deal like Bernie and Annie's. We each have our own little special touches, but the basic pattern remains the same. Now let's map the positive bonding pattern. First we will map Annie and Bernie's and then yours.

Mapping a Positive Bonding Pattern

In mapping our positive bonding patterns, we look for the selves that have taken command of our lives and our decisions. *The questions to ask ourselves are: "Who is driving my psychological car?" "What good mother or good father is operating?" "What good daughter or good son is responding?"* When we map Annie and Bernie's positive bonding pattern, it looks like this:

Annie and Bernie's Positive Bonding Pattern

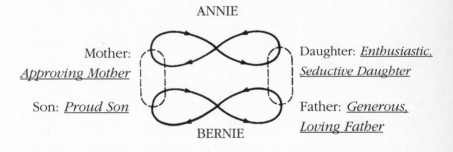

ANNIE

Mother: *Approving Mother*

Son: *Proud Son*

Daughter: *Enthusiastic, Seductive Daughter*

Father: *Generous, Loving Father*

BERNIE

In describing this, we would say that Annie's approving mother is bonded with the proud son in Bernie and that the generous and loving father in Bernie is bonded with Annie's enthusiastic, seductive daughter.

There can be any combination of good parent–good child selves. Your positive bonding patterns will depend upon what your own selves and those of your partner are like. Perhaps there is a coming together of a rational parent who seems to have everything safely under control and a frightened child who is terrified of chaos. Or it may be a nurturing, accepting parent bonding with a shy, insecure, or lonely child. Then, again, it might be a responsible, sensible parent bonding with a disorganized, confused child. *As you learn about these bonding patterns, you learn about yourself, your partner, and your relationship.* Now let's help you map your positive bonding patterns.

BONDING PATTERN EXERCISE 1
Mapping Your Own Positive Bonding Pattern

In this exercise, think about your own relationships and see if you can identify one of your own positive bonding patterns. This bonding pattern can be with your partner or with anyone who is important to you — perhaps one of your own parents or one of your children. As with the disowned self exercises in chapter 2, be sure that you have enough time to do this. Take a deep breath and get centered before you start. You can make your notes on the diagram in the book or copy it onto a piece of paper or into your journal. As you fill in the following diagram, you can use Annie and Bernie's map as a guide.

First, can you feel (or picture) the self in you that loves, protects, feels responsible for, cares for, wants to heal, appreciates, admires, or adores your partner? This is your loving parent, responsible parent, or caretaker self. Name it, or describe something it usually says or does, and fill this in space no. 1.

Next, ask yourself what it is about your partner that makes you feel absolutely safe or appreciated. Can you picture this self in your partner? This is your partner's positive parent self. Give it a name, or write down one of the things it usually says, and fill in space no. 4.

Now, can you picture the child in you who feels good with your partner? Perhaps it is a frightened child that feels safe with your partner; an irresponsible or an incompetent child who feels cared for; an innocent or a needy child who feels protected; or an appreciative child who sees how truly good this partner is. This is the child in you that is involved in this bonding pattern. Name it and fill in space no. 2.

Last, do you have a picture of the little girl or little boy that you can see (perhaps nobody else can) in your partner? It may be sweet or needy, or frightened, or innocent, or helpless. Whatever it is, it is the part that touches your heart. Name it and fill this in space no. 3.

Your Positive Bonding Pattern
YOU

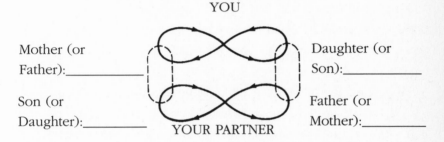

Mother (or Father):_____

Son (or Daughter):_____

YOUR PARTNER

Daughter (or Son):_____

Father (or Mother):_____

How a Positive Bonding Pattern Stops You from Living in Full Partnership

Many of us have grown up using this positive bonding pattern as a map for the perfect relationship. In it, there is no disagreement and no stress. Each partner puts the other first. We remember hearing that "if each of you thinks you are giving to the other about 90 percent of the time, you are probably each giving equally." After all, we were told, "Relationship is about compromise. You must give in order to receive."

There is truth to this folk wisdom. The "me first" approach to life does not work very well when there are two people in relationship whose needs and feelings are to be considered. If both Bernie and Annie were to decide to put their "no more Mr. Nice Guys" in charge, their relationship would suffer. But the positive bonding pattern, although a natural and apparently pleasant way to relate to one another, has its drawbacks.

There is something missing in the positive bonding pattern. A set of selves has taken over the relationship and there is no longer any real choice available to either Bernie or Annie as the default position of the relationship — the bonding pattern — takes control. The partnership is no longer operating. Partnering is a joint venture and both partners must be fully present to make it work. The parent-child selves alone just can't get the job done. Let's look at some of the ways in which we literally lose ourselves when we enter a positive bonding pattern.

In the positive bonding pattern, each partner loses boundaries. Neither can say no to the other. Neither partner can take care of his or her own needs. They blend together, each caring more about the other than about herself or himself. Each is the loving parent to the other. There is no choice.

When we live life in a positive bonding pattern with our partners we each sacrifice ourselves for the relationship. *We give up the parts of ourselves (the selves) that do not fit easily and comfortably into the relationship.* There is a striking image in the fairytale *Cinderella* that illustrates this magnificently. In the story, Cinderella's stepsisters are willing to cut off their toes and heels in order to fit into the glass slipper so that they can win Prince Charming.

On a less dramatic note, but following the same basic principle, Bernie gives up sailing because Annie gets seasick and Annie gives up tennis because Bernie does not like to play. Instead, they take up hiking because they can do this together. It seems, to them, like a small enough sacrifice for the sake of the delicious closeness that they have.

There is something else partners give up when they live in the positive bonding pattern and this is even more subtle. *They lose their ability to react freely to one another. Neither partner can communicate anything that might distress the other.* It is as though they are following an unwritten but inviolable rule. So it is that Bernie must ignore his momentary vulnerability about the finances when he sees Annie's enthusiasm about a new car. If he said to her, "I don't think we can afford a new car, even with your raise," she might get upset. So, instead of reacting freely, he ignores his own feelings to take care of hers. Bernie's generous, loving, responsible father is happy to give Annie whatever will make her happy regardless of the cost.

Negative reactions are absolutely forbidden. All the petty everyday annoyances that crop up in relationships are ignored. Nothing seems important enough to rock the boat. "It's not that important," Annie says to herself as she overlooks the toothpaste tube that is unscrewed or the toilet seat that has been left up. "It's not that important," Bernie says to himself when Annie's sexual response is less than enthusiastic. "What can I expect after so many years?"

Neither partner wants to start an argument. Their own needs or annoyances seem unreasonable or selfish when they are in the positive bonding pattern, so each negative reaction is "swept under the rug." Sooner or later this makes the rug pretty lumpy!

The paradox here is this: When we give up too much of ourselves, we lose the relationship that we are trying to protect. We lose the partnership to which each of us can make our own unique contribution. We have a relationship, it is true, but that relationship is between a few selves — the selves that fit into its limited space.

Again, the goals to strive for are choice and partnership. Where there is choice and partnership, each partner must weigh the opposites and truly feel the pull of the selves in each direction. Bernie must feel the tug of war between his "sailor" who loves the sea and his "loving, responsible husband" who loves being with Annie and cannot bear to leave her at home while he goes out on the boat. Only Bernie can decide which way to go. Annie must feel the tension of the opposites as well. For her, it is between her "tennis player" who loves the sunny days out with her friends and her "pleasing daughter" who wants nothing more than to be with Bernie and make him happy.

In a full partnership, we are able to stand between the self that is irritable and wants to react negatively and the one that wants to keep the peace at all costs. We gradually learn how to disagree and to express our negativity without making the other person wrong. This way, we can bring more of ourselves (and our complexity) into the relationship.

This is not simple. It is not always easy to be a partner. It often feels easier to stay in a positive bonding pattern moving through life on only one leg, the leg that stands in the positive bonding pattern. When we live life as our primary selves dictate, there is no conflict. If Bernie only listens to his loving, responsible father, he will give up sailing without a second thought. If, in contrast, he listens only to his sailor, he will go out sailing without a second thought. Neither is a real choice; neither honors *both* the partnership *and* Bernie's individuality.

When you are able to separate from the positive bonding pattern, the rewards are great. You will have a partnering of equals, each contributing something special to the relationship. Best of all, you can avoid the dreaded negative bonding pattern that follows the positive bonding pattern "even as the night follows the day."

How to Discover the Positive Bonding Patterns in Your Relationship

The most foolproof way to discover that you have been in a positive bonding pattern is to fall into a negative one, which usually happens because positive bonding patterns rarely last indefinitely. The negative bonding pattern is impossible to ignore. We will go into this in detail in a moment. In the meantime, let's look at a couple of less dramatic ways to discover a positive bonding pattern.

In positive bonding patterns everything seems to be going well. If someone asks you how your relationship is doing, you would tell them that it was fine. Things feel very cozy and friendly. You're not aware of the things that are wrong because you love this good feeling you have. People visiting your home would have one of two reactions, depending on their own degree of sophistication. Either they would be mad with jealousy at what a wonderful relationship you have or they would feel as though they were in an airless chamber and were choking to death. *What you must keep in mind in positive bonding patterns is that negativity isn't expressed but neither does it go away.* It simply festers beneath the surface where it keeps building in power.

You also might discover that you are gradually losing track of who you are and what is important to you. You forget what you do like to do and what you do not like to do. (Annie might forget to arrange tennis games until her former partners forget about her, while Bernie no longer seems to find time to get to his boat.) You lovingly and thoughtfully put your partner's needs first and never come up with any ideas, feelings, or reactions that could disturb the status quo. You become more and more fearful of change. "If it ain't broke, don't fix it" could be your motto.

Most frequently, you will find that the passion, particularly the sexual passion, in the relationship has diminished. If you are in a positive bonding pattern, you explain all this to yourself as a normal development in a relationship. It *is* normal, a normal positive bonding pattern. But you may find yourself vaguely dissatisfied. You may even find yourself less than vaguely dissatisfied; you may find yourself yearning for another partner or, at least, for a more exciting life. In positive bonding patterns, fantasies and daydreams tend to go wild. Since such thoughts are unacceptable, you try your best to ignore these thoughts and feel guilty for even having them.

The ability to ignore unpleasantness reaches some pretty exalted heights in positive bonding patterns. We have seen instances when one of the partners has an affair or becomes energetically involved with another person or persons. You might expect this to blow the relationship wide open, as it often does. Sometimes, however, we see the opposite reaction. Everything in the relationship becomes more positive as both partners "understand" and "accept" one another. Even the sexual connection can become more positive under these conditions as both people effectively screen out the feeling that all is not well with them. It is often in this kind of relationship that one partner leaves after many "happy" years and the one who is left is in a state of shock because everything seemed so right. It is only later that she or he begins to notice — retrospectively — all of the little signs that were there along the way that never were dealt with or taken seriously.

In earlier generations, this positive bonding pattern was the ideal. Many of us have known parents, grandparents, or others who lived their entire lives in positive bonding patterns and these worked for them. They lived in a far different world from ours. Their world was far more predictable and did not require the flexibility that the current world demands of us. For most people, the possibility of a partnering relationship did not exist since most relationships were hierarchical and basically patriarchal in nature. (For a detailed discussion of these traditional patriarchal rules for relationship, see Sidra's book, *The Shadow King*.)

The challenge today is to keep what the positive bonding pattern has to offer in terms of loving concern for the partner and a dedication to the relationship and, at the same time, learn to allow our own growth and the growth of the relationship to continue. Do not stop your own life by locking securely into a single set of selves that may no longer be adaptive for either you or your partner.

THE NEGATIVE BONDING PATTERN

If all else fails, you can count on the negative bonding pattern to break the positive bonding pattern. When we say "negative" we do not mean "bad," any more than we meant "good" when we talked about the positive bonding pattern. What we mean is that the negative bonding pattern feels dreadful, simply dreadful. Just as the positive bonding pattern does not allow us to express any negativity toward our partner, the negative bonding pattern does not allow us to express any positive feelings toward them; sometimes it doesn't even allow us to have positive thoughts about our partner. At its most extreme, the negative bonding pattern can lead to separation or divorce. This, however, is not *our* solution of choice for a negative bonding pattern. Frankly, we think that separating from the negative bonding pattern rather than from your partner is a really good alternative. How do you go about this? You learn about your own bonding patterns and work out ways of dealing with them.

The first thing for you to do is to understand that the negative bonding pattern, like the positive bonding pattern, is perfectly normal. *There is nothing wrong or dysfunctional about negative bonding patterns. Everybody has them, even though this doesn't make them feel any better.* As a matter of fact, the negative bonding pattern can feel so bad that you doubt your own ability to function in the world. It may feel so bad that you would rather end the relationship than continue if it is going to cause you to feel this unbearable psychic pain.

The negative bonding pattern usually feels catastrophic, insoluble. It reminds you of how impossible all relationships are. It is an all too familiar pattern! First you learn to trust people and then they, like all their predecessors, disappoint you. At this point, relationship can be so painful that it barely seems worthwhile. This is exactly what happens to Annie and Bernie.

Annie wakes up in the morning to find that her loving Bernie is gone. Instead, she is married to a cold, withdrawn, uncaring man, someone who, now that she thinks about it, reminds her of her father! "That's it," she thinks to herself, "he's just like every other man I have ever met. Men are all alike. They are wonderful and they give you whatever you want until you relax and allow yourself to trust them. Then they know they have you and they change. That's when you get to see what they are really like underneath. They are cold and selfish. Deep down inside men only care about themselves."

Bernie, in turn, thinks to himself, "Isn't that just like a woman? She always gets what she wants. She comes on all sweetness and light and wheedles her way in — taking everything you've got. She never worries about what anything will cost or whether I have to work harder to earn the money to pay for that car! She even has sex with me when she wants something. Women are all alike."

What has happened? The fact is that Bernie is feeling very vulnerable about the new car. Last night, in the positive bonding pattern, he did pay attention to this but, because he is such a fatherly type, he does not know how to communicate his anxiety. It does not fit into his role in life. When we cannot feel and cannot express our vulnerability in relationship we shift into a power mode and suddenly we become withdrawn, judgmental, and possibly punitive. This is exactly what happened to Bernie.

On the other side there is Annie, who is now feeling abandoned and filled with pain at this sudden turn of events. In the positive bonding pattern she also cannot share her feelings of hurt and disappointment and so she, too, moves into power. Annie becomes a very judgmental mother ready to fight it out with Bernie. As far as this judgmental mother is concerned, it is his turn to feel, as the hurt son, the injustice of all of this criticism and, we might add, previous ones as well.

Using the imaginary photos again to give you a picture of the emotional experience of these bonding patterns, let's see what the negative bonding pattern would look like. In the photo on the left-hand side of the frame, we have Bernie. His black hair is slicked back and his green eyes have a cold, cruel gleam in them as he turns his back on Annie and strides away. He looks like an old-fashioned villain. Annie is a blue-eyed, curly-haired blond little girl clinging to his leg and weeping as she tries to keep him from abandoning her.

In the right-hand side of the frame, we have Annie, bigger than life, looking like an angry mother with upraised hand and piercing, angry, all-seeing eyes. Bernie, in this picture, is a terrified little boy, holding up his hand as though to protect himself from her violence, both physical and emotional.

To get the full emotional effect of this bonding pattern on Annie, think of how powerful and cruel Bernie looks through the eyes of the clinging, abandoned little girl. To get Bernie's experience, picture yourself as the little boy trying to shield himself from the huge, powerful mother.

It is interesting to note that each partner is actually experiencing both power over the other and the pain of being hurt. Usually, however, *each partner is more acutely aware of his or her own pain than of her or his power over the other partner.* When you are in a negative bonding pattern like this, you will probably be amazed to learn that your partner has no experience of your pain or helplessness, but instead sees you as immensely powerful, judgmental, punishing, or withholding.

So it is that Annie feels horribly abandoned and hurt and, at the same time, has no idea that Bernie is responding to the criticism of her angry mother self, whether it is implicit or explicit. Bernie, on the other hand, feels his own pain at Annie's attacks and might well be unaware of the impact of his cold, withdrawn self upon Annie.

Whose Fault Is It?

The natural reaction to this pain is to try to figure out who started it or whose fault it is. These negative bonding patterns give each of us the chance to take the moral high ground, a chance to see where the other person has erred or fallen short. Was Annie wrong or was it Bernie? Which of them started this? *In our "no-fault" way of looking at this, neither Annie nor Bernie has made a mistake. Neither of them has started anything.* They were just doing what we humans do.

These negative bonding patterns, just like the positive bonding patterns that often precede them, are what we call "the dance of the selves in relationship." *The bonding pattern is like a dance, a dance that requires two partners. Nobody is ever in a negative bonding pattern alone.* There is good news and bad news about these bonding patterns. The good news is that it is not your fault. The bad news is that it is not your partner's fault either.

We would suggest that, instead of trying to assign the proper amount of blame, Annie and Bernie think of this as the normal progression of a relationship and they map this repetitive pattern as it occurs. Then they can see that there is nothing mysterious, fated, or insoluble about it. It was just a positive bonding pattern that was followed by a negative bonding pattern. You can do the same with your relationships.

Mapping a No-Fault Negative Bonding Pattern

The first step is to find out what part of you is actually participating in the bonding pattern. What follows is a map of the form of the bonding pattern of Bernie and Annie.

Annie and Bernie's Negative Bonding Pattern

ANNIE

Mother: _Angry, Judgmental Mother_

Son: _Frightened, Hurt Son_

Daughter: _Abandoned Daughter_

Father: _Cold, Withdrawn Father_

BERNIE

In describing this, we would say that Annie's angry, judgmental mother is bonded with the frightened, hurt son in Bernie. Furthermore, we would say that the cold, withdrawn father in Bernie is bonded with Annie's abandoned daughter.

As with the positive bonding pattern, there can be any combination of parent-child selves. Among the most popular combinations are: controlling mother and rebel son; cold, withdrawn father and abandoned daughter; rational father and helpless daughter; judgmental mother or father and guilty son or daughter; know-it-all mother and stubborn son; and judgmental father or mother and defensive son or daughter. Your negative bonding patterns will depend upon what your own selves and those of your partner are like. Let's see how the negative bonding patterns show up in your life by taking some time to map one of yours.

BONDING PATTERN EXERCISE 2
Mapping Your Own Negative Bonding Pattern

As with the other exercises in this book, be sure that you have enough time to complete the exercise. Take a deep breath and get centered before you start. You can write on the diagram in the book or copy it onto a piece of paper or into your journal.

In this exercise, we would like you to think about your own relationships and see if you can identify one of your own negative bonding patterns. You can use Annie and Bernie's map to guide you as you did with the positive bonding pattern. As you fill in the following diagram, or map, you will begin to see who each person becomes (or which selves take over) once your negative bonding pattern starts.

First, think of a time when you were displeased with your partner. Can you picture how your adult self felt or acted? Did you judge your partner quietly and withdraw? Did you argue and cast blame? Did you analyze your partner, understand your partner's shortcomings and problems, and then try to discuss them and show your partner what he or she should do next to improve matters? Did you want to punish your partner? Did you try to control your partner? Did you try to fix your partner? Were your reactions different from any of these? Each of these reactions gives a picture of a different self. You can see that there are a lot of options. Give your parental self a name, or describe something it usually says or does, and fill this in space no. 1.

Next, what is it about your partner that makes you feel absolutely unsafe or miserable? Can you picture this self in your partner? Is your partner judgmental, cold, withdrawn, a know-it-all, or invasive? There are many possibilities. This is the negative parent in your partner. Give it a name, or write down one of the things it usually says, and fill in space no. 4.

Now, can you picture the child in you who felt dreadful with your partner? Perhaps it is an abandoned child, a misunderstood child, a frightened child, an incompetent child, a guilty child, a defensive child, or, last but definitely not least, a rebellious child. This is the child in you that is involved in this bonding pattern. Name it and fill in space no. 2.

Last, do you have a picture of the difficult child that you can see in your partner? This, too, can take many forms. It might be a victim, a rebel, or a stubborn child who remains silent but won't listen to a thing you say. It might be a defensive or defiant child that keeps on talking back to you. It might be mute, needy, frightened, guilty, helpless, or inadequate. Name it, or write down something that it says, and fill this in space no. 3.

Your Negative Bonding Pattern

YOU

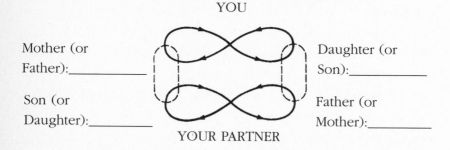

Mother (or Father):_____

Daughter (or Son):_____

Son (or Daughter):_____

Father (or Mother):_____

YOUR PARTNER

Now you have a map of one of your own negative bonding patterns. Congratulations! We spent many interesting and enlightening (we wouldn't exactly say happy) hours diagramming our own bonding patterns in this way. In our relationship, Hal was most expert at becoming the psychological father or the withdrawn and angry father. Whenever he would lose touch with his vulnerability in the relationship, we could count on withdrawal and judgment. Sidra would move in the other direction. She would become very busy, very active, and totally solution oriented until finally something tipped the scale and she would become extremely judgmental. Did we ever have fun with those patterns. And did we ever learn a lot!

Negative Bonding Patterns and Unexpressed Vulnerability

Another major aspect of negative bonding patterns is an under-lying sense of vulnerability. This is what Bernie and Annie could not express to each other. When Annie first saw the car and wanted it, she felt very vulnerable. She had her own conflict about finances even though she was more of a spender than Bernie. She knew how close to the edge they were. She buried her own anxiety and never communicated it to him. Instead she became the child-daughter and he became the father.

Bernie felt very anxious about the money but this got buried as his habitual nurturing father came in and essentially eliminated his anxiety and vulnerability. So, they weren't able to talk about the issue as partners because Bernie and Annie were on holiday while the father and daughter selves took over. This is a normal, every-day type of interaction in relationship. It is no one's fault. The good news is that we can learn to separate from these patterns. *In part-nership the communication of vulnerability becomes a key element. The majority of negative bonding patterns would never happen if the vulnerability were expressed.* First, however, we must learn to feel our vulnerability, which is a most difficult thing to do in a society that values power above all else.

THE CONTENT OF THE BONDING PATTERN: THE DISOWNED SELVES

So far we have looked carefully at two aspects of bonding pat-terns. First, we gave you a picture of what we call the "form" of the bond. We drew diagrams, or maps, of both positive and negative bonding patterns to show you which selves take over. Second, we talked about the underlying vulnerability that ignites the bonding pattern. Now we would like to show you what it is that keeps the bonding pattern burning with such intensity.

It is, however, the primary and disowned selves that keep the bonding patterns burning and give us the ammunition we use when we attack each other. It is the opposites represented by the primary and disowned selves that give us the "reasons" why we are angry with one another in the negative bonding pattern. Whatever we judge or attack in the other person is an expression of a disowned self in us. The more disowned selves that our partner carries and the deeper they are, the more severe will be the attack that we mount. To go back to Annie and Bernie, what would this look like?

For example, Annie is a free spirit in contrast to Bernie, who has a more responsible approach to life. Bernie takes care of the finances and Annie takes care of the house and social life. Annie works as an artist and does not make much money, and Bernie's job involves responsibility for the financial well-being of other people. If we were to contrast their primary selves, it would look something like this:

Bernie's Primary Selves (These are also Annie's disowned selves)	*Annie's Primary Selves* (These are also Bernie's disowned selves)
Responsible	Free Spirit
Business Oriented	Creative Orientation
Work Oriented	People Oriented
Cautious	Takes Risks
Financially Responsible	Financially Irresponsible
Thinking	Feeling

As we look at this list we see a very interesting thing. Bernie's primary selves embody Annie's disowned selves and Annie's primary selves embody Bernie's disowned selves. These differences serve to attract them to each other in the first flourish of love. As they live together, these selves easily become major sources of contention. It is paradoxical that the very things that attract us to our partners — our differences — so easily become the enemies of the partnership and can very effectively destroy it.

In their auto buying conflict, it was Annie's free spirit and feeling selves that wanted the car and it was Bernie's good and responsible self that said yes in the positive bonding pattern. Once their interaction became negative, they attacked each other's disowned selves. Bernie judged Annie for her lack of responsibility and the fact that she never thinks about money. Annie attacked Bernie because he was excessively and compulsively concerned with money and can never just take a risk. This kind of bonding pattern occurs in every relationship. Only the details, the content of the primary and disowned selves, vary.

The work that needs to be done is clear. Annie must learn to embrace more than her free spirit and feeling selves. She must learn to embrace her financially responsible and conservative selves as well. Bernie must learn to broaden beyond his responsible and work-business side and embrace the parts that are more sociable, free spirited, artistic, and creative. Only then can they both stop blaming each other for the holes that exist in themselves and instead use their conflicts as opportunities for learning and growth.

Imagine what would happen if everybody did this. What if, suddenly all over the world, people had to stop whenever they had a judgment or were attacking someone and ask themselves: "Why am I so angry and judgmental? What is it that I am missing so badly in myself that I cannot bear to see it in someone else?" What a different world, what a different kind of partnering it would be. We would see others as mirrors of our missing parts and they would become our teachers rather than our enemies. Groups and nations that carry one another's disowned selves could learn from one another rather than fight one another. If we were all to follow this way of being with others who are different from us, peace on Earth could become a reality rather than an impossible dream.

You have already become familiar with your own positive and negative bonding patterns. How about taking this opportunity to look at the fuel for these bonding patterns. This will show you where your partner is your teacher.

PRIMARY SELF EXERCISE

In this exercise, use what you have learned about primary selves in chapter 2 to make a list of your primary selves and those of your partner. You can use Annie and Bernie's list as a guide. You might even wish to do this with your partner. If you do so, each of you can help the other to identify primary selves.

Your Primary Selves	*Your Partner's Primary Selves*

As you look at this list, you will notice that although some of your primary selves may be similar to your partner's, there are a number of important places where these selves represent opposites. These are the places where your primary selves are the disowned selves of your partner and vice versa. These opposites are the ones that will be fueling your bonding patterns and causing you grief. They also represent the opportunities for growth in your relationship.

IT'S NOT WHAT YOU SAY, IT'S WHO SAYS IT

The lesson in all this work with bonding patterns and the selves is that you are not who you think you are. When you study the patterns that repeatedly emerge in your relationships, you begin to see the selves that get involved in *your* bonding patterns. *You learn that your words are less important than the self that speaks them.* Once you know this, you can extricate yourself from the unending cycle of judgment and blame that characterizes so many of your negative interactions. By recognizing this, and pausing for a moment to consider the bonding patterns that exist and what bonding pattern you may be in at any given moment, you will have greater clarity about your relationships. You will begin to have some choice about which of your selves is speaking. This, in turn, will give you greater control over what happens to you in your relationships.

With this kind of understanding available to you, you can replay the interactions between Annie and Bernie. When Annie asks, "Is anything wrong?" the words sound innocent enough. But you know that when it is her judgmental mother rather than Annie that speaks these words, there is a world of difference in what Bernie feels. He hears that very special tone of voice and reacts as though he has been attacked, which indeed he has.

You see that Bernie, in turn, is not the one answering Annie. It is his withdrawn, judgmental father who speaks the apparently innocuous words "Nothing. I just have a lot of work to do today." Again, the words are innocent enough, but it is who delivers the answer that makes Annie feel abandoned. Both end up feeling dejected, and more conflict is the result. By Bernie and Annie both realizing that it is not the other speaking, but a *part* of the person, they can begin to get to the root of that part's needs and resolve their conflict as partners with a common goal.

THE LESSONS IN THE NO-FAULT RELATIONSHIP

There are three lessons that we learn from a study of bonding patterns. You have learned two of them already and the third will be introduced in the following chapter.

The first lesson is the lesson of the primary and disowned selves that fuel our bonding patterns providing the "reasons" why we are angry. We can think of this lesson as an awakening from the deep enchanted sleep of living in a primary self and an opening of our eyes to the many rich and varied possibilities outside of this self, or selves.

As we have seen, our disowned selves are mirrored by the primary selves of our partner or, for that matter, by many different people in our lives. We know that these are disowned selves because we either judge them or overvalue them. This clearly shows us what it is that we have disowned, what it is that is missing in our lives. These are the selves that our psyches are trying to integrate. Working back from these, looking for what is on the opposite side, we come face-to-face with our primary selves and the rules that have governed our lives.

We are now in a position to separate from our primary selves and to begin the process of integrating the disowned selves. This does not mean that we will ignore our primary selves and *become* our disowned selves; it just means that we can expand and add to our lives the input available from these disowned selves.

The second lesson is learned from the form of the bonding pattern; it is the lesson about who takes over the wheel of our psychological car when we are in relationship. What self is it that does the talking when we fall into a bonding pattern?

Recognizing the selves that take over in the bonding pattern, and learning to separate from them, gives us a way to play our own instruments in our relationships and our partnering rather than be a victim to the repetitive and automatic bonding patterns that entangle us with others. This is a healing of old wounds, a priceless gift.

The third lesson is about what we call "vulnerability." By this we mean our own emotional reality, including both our needs and our sensitivity to others and to the world around us. We have already mentioned that it is unexpressed or disowned vulnerability that ignites the negative bonding patterns. We believe so strongly that an awareness of this vulnerability, and the ability to communicate it, is the key to an emotionally healthy, alive, and intimate relationship, that we have devoted the next chapter to it.

Chapter 4

VULNERABILITY:
THE KEY TO INTIMACY AND BEYOND

From the first time we allowed one another access to what we named the "vulnerable" or "inner" child, a door opened into new realms of relating. As our primary power selves stepped aside and permitted these vulnerable children to communicate their secrets, we discovered a depth of intimacy that we had never thought possible. Up until then there was always a guardian at the door to be sure that what was truly precious or sacred was kept locked away in a safe place, like the basket that held the treasure of the Star Maiden.

W e have been talking at great length about the primary selves. But why are they here and what lies beneath them? Beneath all the impressive, capable, powerful primary selves that we develop over a lifetime, lies our vulnerability. As a matter of fact, it is this that our primary selves were developed to protect. Our primary selves compensate for, and protect, our vulnerability. You can almost think of the primary selves as the warriors that guard the greatest treasure of the kingdom. This chapter is devoted to that treasure — our vulnerability — the key to a healthy and intimate relationship.

Our vulnerability, and the inner child who carries this vulnerability, is the part of us that is closest to our essential being. In the first chapter we spoke of the magical ability, in moments of deepest intimacy, to inhale the fragrance of this essential being. In order to do this, we must separate from our default positions of relating through the selves and reclaim this vulnerability. That is what this chapter is all about.

This vulnerability is carried by a self that we call the *vulnerable child*. This is an inner child that is exquisitely sensitive to its surroundings. It knows who we are. This child is defenseless, but astonishingly perceptive. It approaches others with its heart, not its mind. Actually, it is the absence of defenses that allows this child to tune in to its surroundings so completely and interact so intimately. It responds to the slightest changes in the energetic interactions between people. You may be familiar with author John Bradshaw. Much of his brilliant work with the inner child is about this vulnerable child. Now let's look more closely at this vulnerable child and its key role in relationship.

THE VULNERABLE CHILD

The vulnerable child is a sensitive, usually fairly quiet, child. It is a shy child who observes and only interacts with people when it feels safe. The vulnerable child is very different from other inner child selves that you may have heard about or even worked with. It is definitely not the playful or spontaneous child. It is not the magical child who relates to the magic in the world; this child is usually more solitary than the vulnerable child and prefers to be alone. Nor is it the child who is curious, irrepressible, or rambunctious.

As we grow up, we naturally distance ourselves from this vulnerable child. Our primary selves protect us by burying it. If we lived our lives dominated by our vulnerability, with the vulnerable child as our primary self, we would, indeed, be victims. But, paradoxically, if we have no access to our vulnerability, we do not know *who* we are, *what* we like, and what we *don't* like, we do not know what makes us feel *good* and what makes us feel *bad*. Our lives and the choices we make are controlled by our primary selves and their rules. These choices may have little or nothing to do with what we truly want or need. They are not connected to our souls.

In contrast to this, the vulnerable child gives us valuable information. It lets us know what truly feeds us and what gives us psychic indigestion. But in order to get this information, we must follow an unfamiliar path. We must begin to tune in to the faint indications that something is not right. We must pay attention to these clues rather than try to ignore them as so many of our selves would have us do. When we ignore these clues, we go into the default position.

More About Vulnerability

Now let's look at what we mean when we talk about vulnerability as a feeling state, or a way of being in the world. *Vulnerability, as we use the word, does not imply weakness; it implies openness, sensitivity, and a lack of defensiveness.* So, when we are able to feel our vulnerability, we are able to experience the full range of our reactions to the world around us, the ones that our primary selves usually protect us against. This includes our openness, our finely tuned reactivity to our surroundings, our sensibilities, our physical needs, our craving for intimacy, and all our more sensitive feelings including our loves, yearnings, fears, shyness, insecurities, and discomforts.

When our vulnerability is not available to us, we do not have access to the parts of us that are capable of intimacy. We are, instead, meeting others from our primary selves that fear our vulnerability and feel safe only when we are in a position of power. When it is our primary selves that meet them, we are well protected. You could almost say that we come to others in a full suit of armor.

We approach them from a competitive position, jockeying for power and control, rather than striving for intimacy and partnership. Although this is great if you happen to be going into battle, it is not what you would call a romantic approach to partnering.

In contrast, when we approach our relationships with others with our vulnerability, we bring with us our sensitivities, our feelings, and our ability to relate to another without this overlay of protection. There is a self-awareness and an awareness of the other that brings with it the possibility of intimacy, depth, warmth, sharing, and partnership.

Although we are singing the praises of vulnerability, we do not mean that you should be out in the world vulnerable and defenseless; the world is not a very kind place. So, a brief warning: Do not run out and be vulnerable just yet. We will talk about how you can keep yourself safe by combining vulnerability with power later in this chapter. For now, we would like to give you a picture of what your vulnerability is, how it is carried by your vulnerable child, and the ways in which it manifests itself in your relationships.

THE GIFT OF EMBRACING
YOUR VULNERABLE CHILD

From the first time we allowed one another access to what we named the "vulnerable" or "inner" child, a door opened into new realms of relating. As our primary power selves stepped aside and permitted these vulnerable children to communicate their secrets, we discovered a depth of intimacy that we had never thought possible. Up until then there was always a guardian at the door to be sure that what was truly precious or sacred was kept locked away in a safe place, like the basket that held the treasure of the Star Maiden in chapter 1.

We found that we were able to move beneath surface concerns and into a timeless sacred realm. When this vulnerability was a part of our relationship, or any relationship for that matter, things went well. Whenever we lost this, we lost an essential part of our connection. We felt adrift and alone. And when we struggled and persisted and finally got back the vulnerability, there was magic and we felt as though we were falling in love all over again.

The same was true when we worked with the vulnerable child in others. We found that just about anyone — even a total stranger — who is privileged to see and hear the vulnerable child of another human being is deeply touched. The voice of this vulnerable child is like a tuning fork that elicits a similar vibration in everyone around and creates an immediate and deeply intimate bond. It is a connection that goes beneath all differences and links us to the deepest humanity in one another.

Of course, this is a priceless gift for relationships. We found that when we worked with couples, those who gained access to their vulnerability and were able to communicate it related in a most intimate fashion. Since they knew one another's vulnerabilities, they had a deep understanding, tenderness, and compassion for each other that helped them through the hard times that are a part of the natural ebb and flow of any relationship.

VULNERABILITY AND BONDING PATTERNS

Remember the bonding patterns we talked about in the last chapter? *Without access to your vulnerability, you live life in these bonding patterns. It is the disowned vulnerability — or the lack of access to your vulnerability and the disappearance of your vulnerable child — that triggers the power selves in all bonding patterns, both positive and negative.*

How does this happen? It is really quite simple. If you do not experience your vulnerability, you do not know how to care for yourself properly because you don't know what your real needs are. If you never feel vulnerable, you never have a sense of discomfort that would let you know you need to pay attention to your feelings. You do not even know that you have a need or that something is troubling you! You cannot problem-solve, either on your own or with a partner, because you are not aware that there is a problem. You cannot deal with a difficulty that does not seem to exist.

The alternative to vulnerability is power. When you do not have access to your vulnerability, you automatically move into the default position of the bonding pattern. This distracts you from the underlying vulnerability and gives you a sense of power. The bonding pattern breaks intimacy and focuses your attention on either the needs or the shortcomings of your partner. But intimacy is not all you lose. You also lose the many kinds of support that come with a true partnership.

Returning to the example of Annie and Bernie from chapter 3, we can see how this happens. Bernie thinks of himself as a real man. He works hard at his job in the financial world and plays hard when he plays. He likes to see himself in charge of his life and he takes a great deal of responsibility for others. But Bernie does not like the feeling of vulnerability. He sees vulnerability as a short-coming, some kind of defect. When he was young, he was a shy, sensitive, somewhat fearful child and he felt ashamed of this. From his earliest years, he kept these feelings hidden as best he could. His father and his brothers were very successful and self-assured and Bernie decided that he was going to be like them. He would work hard and be financially successful so that he would never be needy or weak or frightened again.

When Annie asked Bernie about buying a new Jeep, he felt a moment of the old familiar anxiety about money, but he pushed this anxiety away immediately, almost before he was aware of it. As he had done so many times in the past, he ignored — or dis-owned — his vulnerability and moved into a position of power. He was not going to be a frightened child; he was a generous grown man who had all the money he needed (a bit like Santa Claus). This is what triggered the positive bonding pattern where Bernie happi-ly agreed to buy the car. Later, in the middle of the night when he awakened in fear and again pushed away the vulnerable feelings, the bonding pattern turned negative. This time, instead of the powerful, generous father taking over, Bernie became angry and resentful and from this position of power he judged Annie for creating an impossible situation.

How would this be different if Bernie knew about his vulnerability? If he had paid attention to his initial vulnerability, he would have been able to talk with Annie about her idea of buying a Jeep. First of all, he would have known that he felt anxiety about finances and, second, he would have been in a position to express his concerns about buying a new car. He would have included Annie in his deliberations. Together, as partners, they could have reviewed the pros and cons of buying the Jeep.

Like Bernie, we ignore our vulnerability so many times and in so many different ways in our lives! It feels better; we feel more in charge. Our culture encourages us to do this. We must all be supermen and superwomen. Under no circumstances should we give in to any kind of limitation or weakness. Unfortunately, this disowning of our vulnerability, of our own needs, reactions, and sensitivities leaves us unable to truly care for ourselves in our daily lives and, particularly, in our relationships.

HOW TO REDISCOVER YOUR OWN VULNERABILITY

Overlooking vulnerability has been developed into a fine art by most of us. This negation of vulnerability is so much a part of our worldview that we do not notice it either in ourselves or in others. We will help you reverse this process by resensitizing yourself. This involves looking at the clues about discomfort, rather than ignoring them.

To guide you in rediscovering your own vulnerability, we have come up with some questions for you to think about. Feel free to add any others that work for you. You might want to take some time now to sit alone quietly to consider them. Have pencil and paper handy so you can write down your observations. Keep the list with you for a week or so and add to it as you think of other examples.

If you do not like written exercises, just read the questions and see what comes to mind. Try to observe yourself in the coming days — or weeks — and notice when you push beyond your own vulnerability in these ways.

• What are you not doing that you really want to do?
• What are you doing that you really do not want to do?
• When have you done something you did not want to
  do in order to keep the peace?
• When have you passed over something you really wanted
  in order to please the other person?
• When have you pushed past your physical limitations by
  working after you were exhausted?
  skipping meals?
  forgetting to take a break when you really needed one?
  sitting at your desk for hours and hours and hours without once
  changing your position?
  not getting enough sleep?
• When have you ignored your feelings when you were
  loving?
  hurt?
  uncomfortable?
  needy?
  frightened?
  shy?
  overwhelmed?
• What have you decided not to say to your partner because it felt
  too foolish or weak?

These are just a few of the ordinary, everyday ways in which most of us ignore our vulnerability and move into our power selves to cope with the world and to make our relationships work. As you look at these, you will probably find that you have some very special ways that you overlook your own vulnerability. Add them to your list.

These instances of overlooking vulnerability are often pretty innocuous, especially at the beginning. For instance, both of us need to eat regularly. When we get excited about a project, like writing this book, we may forget to stop for lunch. If we do this, we are disowning our vulnerability (our need for food) and you can be sure that we will pay for it later as one or both of us gets irritable and negative.

We are not suggesting that you become weak, self-indulgent, or ineffectual, that you allow your vulnerability to determine your life. We are not suggesting that you allow your vulnerable child to run the show any more than we would suggest that a two-year-old child should make decisions for a family.

What we are suggesting is the idea that the more you know about your vulnerability, the more effective you will be in the long run, both personally and interpersonally. The more you know about your vulnerability, the better you will be able to care for yourself in all areas, from the most mundane to the most spiritual. The more you know about your vulnerability, the more choice you will have in what you do in your life, and your decisions will be more sound than those based solely on power. Last, but certainly not least, the more you are in touch with your vulnerability, the more you will be able to prevent negative interactions, both with your partner and in your other relationships.

TUNING IN TO YOUR OWN VULNERABILITY IN RELATIONSHIP

Tuning in to your own vulnerability in relationship means paying attention to yourself, especially as you experience "little" or "unimportant" disturbances. *Become attuned to what makes you feel good and what makes you feel bad.* What gives you headaches, bad dreams, a stomachache, an allergy attack, a backache, a feeling of uneasiness? What makes you anxious? What are you worried about when you awaken in the middle of the night? What makes you want to get a cup of coffee, or a cigarette, or a drink?

Becoming aware in this way represents a big change for most of us. It also means that when you are talking with someone and suddenly feel abandoned, you pay attention to this sense of abandonment rather than trying to ignore it.

For instance, you and your partner are talking. He thinks of an appointment he forgot but, since he is polite, he does not interrupt the conversation. Instead, he keeps talking. Suddenly, you don't feel good. For no apparent reason, you feel abandoned. Although your partner continues talking with you and does not break eye contact or change position, you sense that something is different, that — despite appearances — somehow your partner has gone away and is no longer present with you.

When you are in tune with your vulnerability, you are sensitive to the quality of the interactions between the two of you. When the connection is altered or broken, you (or a part of you) know(s) about it. However, most of us have learned to ignore our feelings of vulnerability. Your mind tells you that nothing has happened, that everything is fine. And you usually believe it. This time, instead of ignoring your discomfort, pay attention to it.

Look at the situation carefully and try to figure out what is happening and what you want to do about it. *This combines power with vulnerability.* Perhaps you would like to stop the conversation and say something like, "Where did you go?" or "I feel like I just lost you. What's up?" You may be surprised at the answer, which can range from some unspoken reaction like "I did not agree with what you just said" to "I suddenly remembered that I forgot my dentist appointment today." This brings the conversation to a deeper level; you are talking about what is really happening rather than just talking to be polite.

Conversely, you might feel this sense of abandonment and realize that you have stopped paying attention, that you wanted to end the conversation but you were continuing it in order to be polite. With this information, you can gently extricate yourself. You do not have to be cruel, but you do not have to stay in a situation that is unpleasant.

Being tuned in to your vulnerability gives you the chance to know what is really happening inside of you. Say you begin to feel irritable with your son. Instead of trying to figure out what he did wrong, check on yourself. How is it that you feel vulnerable with him? Are you afraid he doesn't love you? Are you afraid that he will not succeed in life and that you will have to support him forever? Do you feel like an inadequate mother (or father) when your friends disapprove of his behavior? Do you love him so much that you cannot set limits and you give him anything he wants? Again, this leads to a deeper consideration of what is unfulfilling in your relationship with your son. You notice what is not working for you and you begin to deal with it directly.

When you are tuned in to your own vulnerability, you become aware of the people who upset you. You realize that there are friends who drain you and give very little in return. You notice that you need to keep your room warmer or that you like the comfort of music playing when you are at home. It just feels better. You walk into a restaurant and an unpleasant hostess gives you a small table next to the rest room and instead of accepting this without complaint, you ask for another table. You do not do this to be mean or assertive. You do it to take care of your vulnerable inner child.

In a relationship, you notice what it is that your partner does that makes you feel bad. You know when your partner does something that shames you or makes you afraid. You do not gloss over this and explain it all away with comments like "She's had a hard day at the office" or "He's just making a joke" or "I deserved that." Your own feelings matter. They really do. As we said when we described the positive bonding pattern, if you do not stay in touch with your own vulnerability and figure out what it is about, you create a distance between your partner and yourself.

If you do not know that you feel abandoned when he is late, or when he ignores you, then you cannot maintain an intimate connection with him. If you do not know that it hurts to have him ignore you at the party and flirt with all the other women, then you will have to withdraw from him. If he frightens you with his anger or shames you with his comments and you ignore this, your vulnerable child will withdraw to protect itself. Your primary self — the one that understands his needs — takes over and takes care of him. This leaves you out of the picture. In order to stay in the picture, you must be vulnerable. In order to stay in the picture, you must be able to feel.

This is the payoff for rediscovering your vulnerability: you and your own needs, feelings, and deepest longings are an integral part of all your important relationships.

COMMUNICATING VULNERABILITY

There is an interesting catch-22 to communicating vulnerability. *You must be able to feel your vulnerability while, at the same time, you feel your power.* Both must be present simultaneously. It is as though you have one arm around a power self and another around the vulnerable child. Keep this principle in mind when you communicate. It takes a while to get the knack of this, but it is possible.

Remember that you are not abdicating to your partner. You are not making your partner responsible for your feelings, needs, etc. You are bringing to your partner the totality of who you are. You are being intimate in a new way.

HELPFUL HINT 1:

If you feel in charge of the situation, you have moved too much to the power side. If you feel that you are at the mercy of the other person, you have become too vulnerable.

HELPFUL HINT 2:

Your partner's reaction will tell you whether or not you have struck a good balance. A balanced presentation usually elicits a balanced, concerned — but not overly responsible — warm response. If your partner becomes judgmental or angry, you have probably moved too far to one side or the other.

As you communicate your vulnerability in this new way, you may notice some differences from your usual ways of being with your partner. See if you can sense in yourself whether it is you — or one of your selves — that is talking. As you speak, remember that your goal is to be received, not to be rescued.

If you do this as we are suggesting, you will have no need of a particular response from your partner because the aim here is to communicate, not to convince. Communicating your vulnerability in this way is communicating from an aware ego; you are standing on two legs, the leg of power and the leg of vulnerability. This will give you a new feeling of stability that is different from the feeling of being in charge.

The communication of vulnerability, without the requirement that your partner assume responsibility for you, is a precious gift. It is in this way that we open to one another the basket of the Star Maiden and allow the other to see all of our most treasured secrets. This brings us to our last consideration about vulnerability. We see vulnerability not as a source of weakness but as the gateway to the soul.

VULNERABILITY — THE GATEWAY TO THE SOUL

There are tears of sadness that everyone knows about. But there are other tears, those that well up, unbidden, when we feel deeply, when our hearts and souls are touched. We have named these "the tears of the heart." When these appear in our eyes, it does not mean that we are unhappy, weak, or overwhelmed. It just means that our deepest vulnerability is available and that it has been touched by either human or divine energies.

Tears have usually been taken as a sign of weakness or self-indulgence and most of us have done our best to avoid them at all costs. So it is that when our eyes begin to tear, we are ashamed of ourselves and stop whatever feeling is producing these tears. We literally turn off our vulnerability and the accompanying human reaction to being deeply touched. When we do this, we deprive ourselves of a sacred experience.

We have spoken to numberless vulnerable inner children in our day, and many of these sessions were observed. Invariably, the observers were deeply touched and we noticed that a large percentage of them found that tears flowed while they watched and listened. This did not mean that they felt sad or were sorry for the vulnerable child that was speaking. It meant that they were deeply touched. We suggest that if you are emotionally moved and tears come to your eyes, do not tense up, just let them be. They will not overwhelm you. Know that these are not a sign of frailty, know that they are the priceless tears of the heart.

We wonder if the ancient Romans knew about these tears. Among the prized possessions that have been found in tombs, there are many beautiful, delicate lachrymal vases. These are supposed to have collected tears of mourning. But suppose, just suppose, that these vases were not for tears of sadness but were, instead, for tears of the heart.

Perhaps in ancient times they knew that these tears and our vulnerability were precious, that they connect us with the deepest humanity in one another, the place in which we touch the divine. And, knowing this, perhaps they included these tears for the journey to the afterlife because they believed these tears were a gateway to the soul.

Let's take a moment to review the importance of vulnerability in relationship. First, it is our vulnerability that brings our soul reality into relationships. Without it, our connections tend to lack real intimacy and depth. With it, we incorporate the treasure of the Star Maiden. Second, an awareness of our vulnerability gives us the ability to learn about ourselves and to know what is good and what is not good for us; this allows us to see the steps we must take to make our relationship a healthy one. Third, as we become aware of the vulnerable child within us, we learn to care for it ourselves in a conscious and thoughtful way rather than expecting our partners to assume full responsibility for it. Lastly, as we learn about our vulnerability and how to communicate it, we will spend less and less time in bonding patterns, the default position of relationship.

As we allow vulnerability to become a part of our lives, we are able to make an ever-deepening connection to others. This connection is not only an emotional connection, it is an energetic connection as well. In the next chapter we will teach you about this energetic connection and its importance in all your relationships. We will show you what it is, how it operates, and how you can use it with choice.

Chapter 5

THE MAGIC OF LINKAGE: ENERGETIC CONNECTION AS A HEALING FORCE

When we link energetically with choice and awareness, a soul connection is made. We begin to develop a new kind of sensing in which the visible and invisible worlds become as one. It is in the silence of this linkage that we are able to open the basket of the Star Maiden and find the riches that lie within it.

Think back for a moment to the time when you first met your partner, or anyone else that you felt very close to. Do you remember what it was like? Do you remember the warm glow in your body and especially in your heart? When we fall in love and feel this warmth and sense of connection, we often use language that is energetically based. We may say in describing the person that he or she has such beautiful energy. When someone asks us what we see that is so great in the other person, we may say that we can't really describe it except that the "vibes" are so great between us. We may say about someone who enters a room that they have a charismatic quality and that we can feel the power they generate.

When we feel these kinds of feelings in our connection to some-one, it is based on a combination of psychological, emotional, physical, spiritual, and energetic factors. We are used to dealing with the first four of these. Relationship as an energetic event, however, is a new kid on the block and involves a new kind of aware-ness of relational issues.

The term *linkage* refers to the energetic connection between people. An "energetic" connection is made with a particular kind of energy, specifically the energy of body. The knowledge of the body's energy fields is an ancient one. For millennia traditional Chinese medicine has focused upon the energy systems within the body. They see this body energy, or *chi,* as moving through our bodies along energy meridians much as our blood runs through our circulatory system.

These energy fields are not limited to the boundaries of our physical bodies, however. They extend beyond our physical bod-ies and (like ultraviolet light) are usually invisible to the naked eye. Many of the most effective Asian martial arts make use of these body energy fields to enhance the power of the individual. It is these energy fields and these streams of energy that we are talking about when we speak about energetic connections.

We are sure that you have experienced this, even if you did not have the words to describe what was happening. For instance, have you ever felt a warmth or coolness when you were with somebody? That is an experience of the other person's energy field. With some people it seems as though they are standing very close and you might even feel the need to step back a bit despite the fact that there is already some distance between you. That would mean that the person was extending his energy field and touching you with it, perhaps even enveloping you. Then there are other times when you can actually be talking with someone and you suddenly feel alone even though the conversation has not ended. This would be an indication that the other person has withdrawn her energy field and you are, indeed, alone.

Linkage is about the interactions of these energy fields. It is closely related to the term *intimacy* but it is not exactly the same. Intimacy carries with it the idea of a certain kind of closeness between people. This closeness can be in different areas. People can be physically intimate, emotionally intimate, intellectually intimate, psychologically intimate, spiritually intimate, or any combination of these. In most instances, intimacy also carries with it an energetic connection.

There are exceptions to this, however. One exception would be two people who feel extremely intimate in an intellectual way while sharing ideas and concepts but who have no energetic connection at all. The same might be true of two people who feel psychologically intimate but who have no energetic connection accompanying this. In both of these exceptions, people may talk for hours and spend vast amounts of time together but have essentially no energetic connection. There is no energy field between them; the air between them is cool rather than warm and full.

Generally speaking, the selves within us that support our ability to use power in the world and become successful are not accompanied by energetic linkage. This would include the part of us that imposes rules on our behavior, the one that operates in a controlling way, the mind, the responsible self, the perfectionist, the pusher, and the critic. The selves that support linkage have to do with our ability to *be* rather than to *do*. They would be the selves that have a connection to our vulnerability and feelings, to our sensuality, and to our soul reality.

We usually find that partners are opposites in terms of how open (linkage) or closed (nonlinkage) they are energetically. We want to make it very clear that we have no judgments about whether being open or closed is good or bad. There is a popular misconception in psycho-spiritual thinking that being open is good and being closed is bad. Nothing could be further from the truth. What we are interested in is helping you to have a choice as to how open or closed you are at any particular time. It is *choice* that gives us freedom, not simply being energetically available to everyone around us. Why don't we look at an example of a couple in relationship and see what this looks like.

Marie and Alice are partners but they are quite different in many ways. Marie loves to make contact with everyone and feels very open to everyone. Energetically speaking, she is linked in all of her contacts with people and if she doesn't feel that the other person is open to her she feels quite lost and quite unable to handle that person. Generally what she does in this situation is become even more open and personal, which makes the person she is with withdraw because she or he is too overwhelmed. Marie is very judgmental toward people who are less open than she is despite the fact that Alice, her partner, is her polar opposite in this respect.

In our way of looking at this, we would say that Marie is someone who is identified with "personal energy." Not surprisingly, someone like Marie will invariably come together with a person like Alice who is not at all open energetically, who holds herself back both psychologically and energetically, and who tends to be much more "impersonal." This is one of the most frequent combinations of opposites that we find in relationship and it causes no end of trouble between partners until they both learn about these energies. Each partner must learn how to access both systems, the personal and the impersonal, in his or her own life and in relation to each other.

For instance, Marie and Alice love each other but, despite this, they judge each other for being too open or too closed. Since we always judge our disowned selves, they will continue to judge each other until each of them begins to develop the missing quality that her partner carries.

Another common pair of linkage/nonlinkage opposites are what we call "being" energy and "doing" energy. Here, too, we find in most relationships that there is one person who tends to be more identified with being and one who tends to be more identified with doing. Being energy is associated with energetic linkage and doing energy is usually associated with either impersonal energy or sometimes with a complete withdrawal from any kind of energetic contact at all.

You can have a being energy when you are alone or when you are with another person or persons. Some people have it when they are alone but cannot have it with another person. Being energy is a very important kind of energy because it allows us to rest into our partners. It is like being able to move vertically as well as horizontally, inward as well as outward. Doing-energy people must always move horizontally, which stops them from being able to experience any kind of deeper intimacy with other people. If we cannot experience this deeper connection with our partner, then we are in trouble because we are missing something important. It is the deep kind of connection that feeds us.

When you think about the many selves, remember that within each person there are two sets of selves. In one set, there are those selves having to do with being successful in the world such as the power self, the pusher, the inner critic, the perfectionist, and the achiever. These selves do not create energetic connections or require intimacy because they are always moving horizontally and their job is to make a person successful and safe and powerful.

In the other set are the selves that are concerned with linkage and with intimacy such as the vulnerable child, the sensual and sexual selves, the soul self, and the spiritual self if it is heart-based rather than mentally based spirituality. It is amazing how in relationship these two sets of opposites find each other. We need them both. This chapter is about learning how to use both sets of selves so that we have personal and impersonal, linkage and nonlinkage, intimacy and nonintimacy available to us by choice whenever we need them.

Why Is Energetic Linkage So Important?

Linkage feeds us. It fills us up and makes us feel good. Without it we feel as though we're starving to death. We must get our linkage one way or another and people get it in the most amazing variety of ways. Some people even pour their energy into inanimate objects that cannot respond.

If we do not create our primary linkage in our primary relationship, then it will go somewhere else. In families with children, the linkage will go to one or more of the children and they become the de facto marriage partner. It may go to a friend or friends or to work or to your computer. It may go to your dog or cat or to food or to alcohol or to television. The list is endless.

When there is no energetic linkage in the partnering process, people are particularly open to other romantic attractions. This is very common. These linkages might remain a fantasy, and some people spend hours thinking about either a special someone or several someones, picturing what it would be like to be with them. Other people make extremely strong energetic connections that do not cross the line into romantic attachments. And sometimes the energetic linkage moves out of the realm of fantasy and/or friendship and the person actually has an affair.

Even in your primary relationship, however, the idea is not to always be totally open and available and personal. The idea is to have a choice about how much or how little linkage you wish to have at any moment. There will be times when you crave linkage and times when you need space.

Let's say that you are the kind of person who is very open and energetically available to everyone. So long as you are with people who are equally open to you, things go well. What happens when you must go to a business lunch with a colleague, someone who is a colder kind of person and much more impersonal? You would have a very difficult time. You try to be very personal, desperately wanting to make energetic contact even as you present your plans for a new fund-raising project. When he does not respond personally, you would become more and more nervous and self-conscious because you know that something is not working. You would simply not know what to do next. The other scenario, of course, is that you would find this person absolutely irresistible, fall madly in love, and marry him. Then you have plenty of time to learn about link-age and work it all out in the relationship.

Imagine now that you are in the same situation presenting your fund-raising project, but that you suddenly have the ability to reg-ulate your energies and that you can choose how open or closed you are energetically. Now you can stop trying to make energetic contact and, instead, you turn down your energy toward a more impersonal mode. By doing this you are able to deal with this very impersonal fellow at lunch. It will not be a case of one primary self talking with an opposite primary self.

Sidra describes this as learning to play your own energetic instrument. In partnering it is very valuable to be able to do this. For instance, if Marie remains personal and continues to judge Alice for being too aloof and impersonal, and if Alice remains impersonal and continues to judge Marie for being too open and personal, then we have the basis for big trouble.

If Marie and Alice can both learn how to play their own ener-getic instruments, then they have an entirely new way of being with one another. They each can make choices about how open or closed they will be based upon their own individual needs as well as the needs of the partner. What a difference this can make!

In our work with couples, the issue of linkage is central. It is the cornerstone of our work. The first step is learning to recognize whether or not linkage is present. Do you know when there is an energetic connection between you and your partner or between you and anyone else? Can you recognize this?

RECOGNIZING LINKAGE

Linkage is not some vague and esoteric idea. Energetic connec-tions are happening or not happening all the time and there are a large number of people who recognize these energies on a natural and intuitive basis. Say your partner tells you that she loves you. You are happy that she says this but you have a feeling of discom-fort. Something is off. The words are right, but the sense of contact is not there. From our standpoint the linkage is not there and you sense its absence.

Then you ask your partner if anything is wrong; you say that you appreciate her expression of love but that something is not quite right. If your statement does not threaten her, she might say a number of different things to you. She might tell you she is pre-occupied with work. She might tell you that she met someone recently and felt attracted to that person. She might say that she is bothered by the fact that you are always busy and she spends a great deal of time trying to make contact with you. She might say that she does not know what you are talking about.

The point is that when you are aware of energetic linkage you know when someone is in contact with you and when this contact is missing. Otherwise you might feel like there is something wrong with you because you can't accept her words of love when the energetic reality has nothing to do with them. When you *know* about energetic linkage, you know that the words "I love you" simply do not match her withdrawn energy field.

In our everyday language we hear people use such expressions as: he has great vibes; she's so charismatic; I really like your energy; I feel so connected to you; they really make great music together. These are all statements about energy fields and energetic linkage. One of the reasons why the energetics are often ignored or even avoided is that the energetic reactions so often become sexualized. If you sit across from your partner and begin to feel this energetic connection, it feels really good. This good feeling tends to build and, before you know it, you feel sexual. If you act on this very quickly, you might have great sex but you may well lose the experience of the ongoing linkage.

Sexual linkage is not the same as the kind of energetic linkage that we are talking about. There are couples who have very active and very positive ongoing sexual relations who have not one iota of energetic linkage when they are not having sex. This is one of the reasons why so many people experience a sense of loss and emptiness after orgasm. If energetic linkage is not present after the orgasm, then it most likely is not present in the relationship in general and the yearning for this linkage persists.

The idea of linkage is based on the fact that we all have an energy field around us that emanates from our physical body. This is a strange idea to most people born and raised in societies of the Western world. It is a much more familiar idea to many cultures of the Far East. Over the past twenty-five years a great deal of innovative healing work has been developed in the West in which practitioners work with energy meridians such as those found in acupuncture and acupressure as well as the energy fields outside of the body.

Here, however, we are not focusing on working with energy fields from the standpoint of healing. Instead we are looking at energetics from the standpoint of physical consciousness and the need to learn to have more effective and conscious control of the energetic linkage in our relationships.

The first step is to learn to recognize when linkage is present and when it is not present. Then you can learn how to control the linkage so you can have a real choice about how much or how little intimacy you wish to have in any situation. In order to do this, we have designed some exercises for you to do with a partner to (1) help you become familiar with linkage and (2) learn how to use it in a more conscious way.

If you don't have a partner, or your partner doesn't wish to do these exercises, you can enlist the help of a friend. These energetic interactions occur in all relationships, and you can learn a lot by doing the exercises with someone who isn't your "significant other." As a matter of fact, it might even be easier to practice with someone other than your significant other in the beginning.

As you begin to work with energetic linkage, please remember that this is easier for some people than for others and don't be discouraged if it sounds a bit difficult. Do you remember how we talked about primary selves acting as default positions? People have two basic default positions. One is related to thinking and the other is related to feeling (including feeling the energies we are talking about). If your default position is one of feeling, you are probably aware of the energetic aspects of interpersonal interactions already, in which case you will find that these ideas and the following exercises come pretty naturally to you. You already have the proper software installed to read the energetic information that comes in.

If, on the other hand, your default position is more mental and your mind is paramount in all your life's dealings, you might not have developed much conscious awareness of these energies even though you are reacting to them on a daily basis. You just don't have the software to read what is happening and to register your reactions. You need new software installed to allow you to understand this energetic input because you cannot do so with your mind. It's like trying to insert complex graphics into a financial program; there's no place to put them. If there's some difficulty at first, just remember all the awkwardness when you add new software to your system. Once it gets going, it's worth all the trouble!

Now try to relax and trust whatever happens in the process. If you prefer not to do the exercises or can't do them for any reason, just read through them so that you can get some idea about how linkage works.

THE LINKAGE EXERCISES

To prepare for the following exercises, set aside at least one half hour for each exercise during which you and your partner can work together without being disturbed. You can do them one at a time, or do them all in one sitting. Just make sure that you are in a private space where you will not be interrupted and allow plenty of time for the exercises so you won't feel pressured and will have enough time for discussion.

Choose a quiet, comfortable place indoors away from drafts and noise so you can concentrate on your linkage without distraction.

Try not to think very much. Instead, relax and pay attention to any sensations of warmth and subtle changes in your feelings. Wearing comfortable clothing and no shoes also helps to focus your attention on the exercise and minimize discomfort. Arrange two similarly sized chairs opposite one another for each of you to sit on.

To begin, appoint one of you Partner A and the other Partner B. Then be seated across from each other with about two or three feet between you. This exercise will be done with your eyes open. Read these instructions aloud or have someone else read them to you as you do the exercise.

LINKAGE EXERCISE 1
Learning to Extend and Withdraw Your Energy

Imagine that your spine is at the center of an energy field that runs up and down your body. From this core you can extend your energy outward toward your partner or anyone else. You can also withdraw your extended energy and pull it back into the core of the spinal column. We know how difficult it is to imagine extending your energies toward another person and also withdrawing it. What is important to realize is that you are doing this all the time anyhow. It is just that you are unconscious of doing it.

To get a sense of what this feels like, imagine a situation where you and your partner are sitting together and suddenly your partner says to you, "Where have you gone? You've disappeared!" You are not even aware that this has happened, but your partner is. Perhaps your partner has said something that upset you and hurt your feelings, but you weren't aware that your feelings were hurt. So you *withdrew your energy* from your partner without even being aware that you did it. Then the doorbell rings and it is someone you like very much and suddenly you *extend your energy* to that person and you have no idea that you are doing it. Your partner picks up on it though and mentions to you later how open you were to your friend and how closed you were to him or her.

Now, let's be brave and plunge into this unknown but fascinating world and learn to take control of our energetic instrument so that we can play it rather than allowing it to continue playing us, which it is, in fact, doing all the time.

In this first exercise you will extend and withdraw energy as we direct. You can imagine that your spine is like a flower that is exuding a lovely fragrance toward the other person. Or you can imagine that you are sending a cloud of warmth, light, or color, or a current of electricity, toward your partner. Some people prefer to use their heart as the center point. If this works for you, imagine that you have a flower, a glowing golden light, an electric current, a warmth, or even a spray of water or a sound moving from your heart to your partner. When you withdraw energy you simply pull back whatever kind of energy you have been sending.

1. *Extend energy*. Extend your energy toward each other. Feel yourself and picture yourself blending with your partner. Feel the warmth that occurs when you blend in this way. As you feel this sense of connection to your partner you will feel warmer and you will have a sense of intimacy and closeness. This is the feeling that comes with energetic linkage.

2. *Withdraw energy*. After thirty to sixty seconds, pull back your energy and feel the vacuum that is left. It feels like a complete emptiness. The feeling of warmth and connectedness is no longer there. People often experience the space between partners as being cooler than before. The intimacy is gone.

3. *Repeat* these two steps two or three times and practice them for a number of days in a row.

After each round of the exercise is over, take your time and talk with each other about your experience. It is very valuable to give each other feedback because you are literally training each other in the recognition of linkage.

Pay attention to how you react to the energy linkage and withdrawal. This is an energetic occurrence only, but it usually has some emotional component. This emotional reaction varies. Most people like the energetic connection, but there are a sizable number who feel this is a bit too much and are relieved when the energy is withdrawn. Some people react with discomfort when the linkage is withdrawn. Some people, even when they know that this is an exercise, have the feeling of abandonment, or even a momentary feeling of "What did I do wrong?" when the partner's energy is withdrawn from them. What are your reactions? What thoughts enter your mind? What feelings appear?

LINKAGE EXERCISE 2A
Partner A Learns to Regulate Energy

In the first exercise, we showed you how to create an energetic linkage, how to turn it off, and how to recognize its presence or absence. Now we will show you how to regulate it.

Before you start the next exercise, we want you to imagine that you have in your hand a dial that regulates energy. Design it in your own way. It has controls that allow you to turn your energy up or down, to make it stronger or weaker, or more personal or less personal. Remember that energy follows thought. Our ability to use our minds properly and also to use our imaginations can help us create and experience the reality of energetic contact.

1. *Partners A and B withdraw your energy fields* as in exercise no. 1, step 2.

2. *Partner B remains withdrawn*. B continues to hold back his or her energy and remains in a neutral position.

3. *Partner A increases energy*. Partner A now uses the (imaginary) regulating device and opens up his or her link-

age as strongly as possible. Partner B simply receives it and remains neutral, but B can let A know what he or she is feeling.

4. *Partner A decreases energy.* After about thirty to sixty seconds, A turns the energy down. Do this slowly and feel the control that is possible. You are now moving the energy from personal to impersonal, from warm to cool.

5. *Partner A increases energy.* When the linkage is gone hold this for thirty to sixty seconds and then bring the linkage in again, as decisively as possible. It is best to do this slowly as a way of developing mastery.

6. *Partner A decreases energy to a comfortable level.* After thirty to sixty seconds reduce the warm personal energy you have been sending to Partner B and find a level of linkage that is comfortable for you, somewhere between personal and impersonal. This is your natural comfort space at this moment. You can always change it.

After you have finished take time to talk with each other. You can repeat this exercise as many times as you wish.

LINKAGE EXERCISE 2B
Partner B Learns to Regulate Energy

Repeat the previous exercise, reversing the roles of Partners A and B. Follow the same directions, only now it is Partner B who is learning to regulate the energy flow and Partner A who remains neutral. Be sure to take time for discussion.

So far we have done the most basic exercises of energetic training. You have begun to learn to recognize when someone is sending energy to you and when it is being pulled away, when there is a field and when there is not a field. You have also learned that you can regulate your own energy system and increase or decrease linkage at will.

In the next two exercises you will learn another skill. Suppose that you are with someone who is inundating you with energy. This person loves to be wide open energetically all the time and has no control or choice about linkage. Imagine that this person is 100 percent personal. Ordinarily in this kind of situation you do not have many options. You can collapse into this person and blend energetically, or you can withdraw as best you can and get away as soon as possible. This happens constantly in our interactions. We just don't know that it is happening. After the next exercise you will have a third option that allows you to change the intensity of this energy as it comes toward you.

LINKAGE EXERCISE 3A
Partner A Learns to Handle Invasive Energy

In this exercise Partner B will do his or her best to swamp and overwhelm Partner A with energy. Partner A will practice dealing with this energetic barrage by turning down the linkage as in the last exercise. As A turns the linkage down, the energy field between you will become more impersonal and a bit cooler. Then A will turn his or her energy up and down a few times and finally find a comfortable level of energetic interaction.

1. *Withdraw energy.* Begin by pulling back your energy fields and withdraw your energy into the core of your body.

2. *Partner B opens up energy field.* Partner B extends his or her energy and opens up the linkage as strongly as possible to try to swamp and overwhelm Partner A energetically.

3. *Partner A cools energy field.* After thirty to sixty seconds, Partner A will begin to turn the linkage down slowly, creat-

ing a more impersonal connection. Partner B continues to send as much warm, open energy as possible. Both A and B will begin to feel a more impersonal connection.

4. *Partner A opens up field.* After thirty to sixty seconds, Partner A will open the linkage again and gradually turn up the power of the linkage until it is very strong again.

5. *Partner A establishes comfortable level.* After thirty to sixty seconds, Partner A again turns down the volume of the personal linkage until it reaches a point where he or she is comfortable with the balance between the personal and impersonal energies. This is how Partner A learns to make a clear choice about the level of intimacy desired at any particular time regardless of the requirements and desires of the other person involved.

6. *Take time to talk about what happened and how you felt.*

LINKAGE EXERCISE 3B
Partner B Learns to Handle Invasive Energy

Repeat the last exercise but reverse partners. This time Partner B will be regulating the energy as Partner A tries to be as energetically invasive as possible. Take time to discuss what happened and how you felt when you are through. We strongly recommend that you repeat these exercises several times on different days to get more practice. You can also try them with more than one partner to see how it feels with different people.

THE NEW INTIMACY

What we have done in linkage exercises 1 through 3 is lay the foundation for a new kind of intimacy. In the first exercise you learned to create an energetic linkage and to recognize its presence and absence. In the second exercise you learned to open up your energy field so that you are more personal (warm and open) and to close it down so you can be more impersonal (cool and objective). In the third exercise you discovered that you can neutralize the energy field between another person and yourself by simply adjusting your own field. So if you are being swamped by someone, or you feel invaded energetically, you neither have to blend with that person nor run away from them; all you have to do is turn your own energy field up or down until you find your comfort level.

In the old form of intimacy, two people come together with their warm, personal energy fully open. They blend with each other energetically as well as psychologically. In some systems of psychology this is called *fusion*.

In the new form of intimacy, we use what we call the *aware ego*. This means that intimacy is no longer defined by energetic closeness and a fully open energy field, but rather by an energetic linkage that permits choice. You remain totally present and energetically connected, but you have the ability to regulate the level or intensity of the energetic interchange between your partner and yourself. It is this kind of choice that gives you real freedom. You are separate individuals who can come together as you wish.

In the last exercise, you will practice being together in "being" energy. This is a particularly intimate (but not necessarily sensual) way of contacting your partner. It is an energetic connection that makes a space for your vulnerability, or the vulnerable child, to contact another human being.

LINKAGE EXERCISE 4
Learning to Be Present in "Being" Energy

Sit facing each other with about two to three feet between you. It is particularly important to schedule a minimum of a half hour with no interruptions for this exercise. The room you use should be totally private. "Being" energy is the ability to *be* with another person without having to *do* or *say* anything. In this space you will feel your mind and your pusher self wanting to interrupt because they do not see any point to "being." They only want to "do." Feel free to tell your partner what your mind or your pusher self is saying while you remain in the being state.

1. As each of you settles in, find your personal energetic comfort level between personal and impersonal and sit with one another in this energetic linkage. Remind yourself that there is nothing to do and no place to go. Just allow yourself to *be*. You will find that a fairly strong energy field develops between you when you do this for a while. If it gets too strong for one of you, just turn the field down as you did in exercise 3.

2. Allow yourself to speak out loud the thoughts or feelings that come up. When you have this kind of energetic connection and you talk, the talking is not linear. There is no pressure to understand anything, to accomplish anything, or to fix anything. You are here just to hang out together in an open and comfortable energetic field.

In the beginning you may stay this way for five or ten minutes. Later you may wish to stay together for longer periods.

Notice how slow and quiet your communication becomes. Verbal communication in this space is totally different from regular talking. We sometimes refer to it as "champagne talking" because it is as though the ideas and thoughts bubble up from the toes and through the mouth and idea number one need have no connection to idea number two.

3. Decide when to complete this exercise and plan when you are going to practice it again.

"Being" Together

This way of "being" together is usually a profound experience for couples. So often a couple will say that this is how it was when they first met and that sometime, somehow, somewhere it just disappeared and was replaced by all the demands and duties of daily life. Remember how wonderful it was to just hang out together? Practicing this being energy with each other on a regular basis is a way of deepening your intimacy. This is different from going for a walk or reading together or watching a sunset together. In this way of being together you are facing each other with no music, no television, no agenda, just two people allowing their natural energies to mix and accepting whatever might happen. It is truly a way of learning to flex one's intimacy muscles.

When you do this you are experiencing a very different aspect of relationship, one in which the energetic reality is much more important than the reality of the mind and its many words. This does not mean that we do not value the mind. Not at all! What we want to do is to bring balance to the mind. Your mind cannot create linkage and cannot understand linkage. So we must learn to bring balance to the psychic system by having the mind and words on one side and the being energy and other energetically based selves on the other. The mind can never see what is in the box of the Star Maiden. It is only when we have access to our being energy and to our vulnerability that the box is no longer empty but filled with the special delights that are invisible to all but the heart.

What you have accomplished in this series of exercises is really quite profound. By the time you master these exercises, you will know what it feels like when an energy field is or is not present between you and someone else. When your partner says I love you, you will know whether or not there is an energetic connection that goes with this statement. If the connection isn't there, it is time to find out why.

You will also learn to regulate your own energies so that you can adjust how personal or impersonal you wish to be as well as how much or how little being energy you wish to have available for others. You have in fact already begun to develop an ability to practice the new intimacy in which you have the chance to make clear choices about how much or how little intimacy you wish to have at any moment in time.

RENEWED INTIMACY: AH, TO LOVE LIFE!

Once they've tasted it, most couples agree that they would do almost anything to regain the timeless intimacy that can be generated by the energy that flows between partners. This linkage is what relationship is all about. It is where a very deep feeding occurs and it is where souls touch. Once it is possible to meet in this "being" energy, it is also easier for partners to begin to communicate the vulnerability.

Partnering leads us inexorably to this kind of connection. It is what makes the difficult times worthwhile. It is the payoff for all the work, all the study, all the learning, and all the negative bonding patterns. It is the reason that we have to learn about the selves and how to separate from them. It is why we cannot live our lives with an out-of-control primary self like the pusher or the critic. It is why we have to learn about bonding patterns. Without all of this work and experience we cannot even find this linkage, let alone maintain it.

If you have a strong inner critic that is pounding you mercilessly on the head, how can you possibly sit quietly with a partner? There is no silence. Not when you have such a critic inside screaming at you like a radio that is playing ten times too loud. If you have an out-of-control pusher, how can you possibly slow down long enough to sit quietly with a partner? There is just too much to do. Your pusher keeps listing what has to be done even as you sit and try as hard as you can to enter into a being state. Again, there is no silence. If you are dominated by a pleaser that is committed to pleasing your partner full time, how can you quietly rest into each other? You cannot. Your pleaser will want to be sure that you are doing linkage properly and will be focused constantly on how your partner is feeling about you and whether or not she or he is approving of you.

If you are married to money or to your computer, how can you possibly take enough time away from your business or the Internet to just sit? If you are energetically married to your children rather than to your partner, how can you possibly be separated from them to spend this kind of time with a partner? The list is endless. The answer is simple. You must learn about your selves and how they interact with your partner's selves. As you unhook from the ways of being that are dictated by these different selves, you will begin to discover the kind of intimacy we all yearn for, the intimacy that most of us knew when we first fell in love.

When we link energetically with choice and awareness, a soul connection is made. We begin to develop a new kind of sensing in which the visible and invisible worlds become as one. The world of spirit begins to open to us through the path of relationship. As we have just commented, it is in the silence of all of these linkage energies that we begin to see the sparkles and fairy dust and magic and spirit that inhabit the box of the Star Maiden.

So far in section 1 of this book we have covered what we consider the fundamental building blocks of relationship. We have helped you discover your many selves and showed you how these selves interact with your partner's selves in the bonding patterns. We have also introduced you to the energetic realities of relationship. In section 2 we explore some specific aspects of relationship and life circumstance and apply these basic principles to these areas. What better place to begin phase two of our journey than in the area of sexuality and the role that it plays in the partnering process?

SECTION 2

ENHANCING RELATIONSHIP

Chapter 6

PASSIONATE PARTNERING: SEXUALITY AND SENSUALITY BEYOND THE BEDROOM

A comprehensive and satisfying sexuality in partnering does not start and end in the bedroom. You cannot separate your physical relationship from the totality of what happens between you as partners in the other aspects of your life.

So far we have been dealing with basics. We spoke of the many selves that live in each of us and that determine so much of what happens in relationships. You learned about bonding patterns as an expression of the interaction of these selves between partners. You learned about vulnerability and how central it is to all relationships to develop a conscious connection to this vulnerability. We also introduced you to the idea of energetic linkage and how important it is to the partnering process. Keep these new ideas in mind as we consider sexuality and relationship.

We have seen many hundreds of couples over the past twenty years. In many instances, sexuality is cited as presenting a problem, or at least it is a matter of primary concern to one of the partners. It is with sadness and sometimes with wonderment that we listen to these stories. The sadness we feel is the intense pain that partners experience when their sexuality isn't working. Our wonderment comes at what, to us, is the often complete lack of connection between the two people on so many different levels. How on earth could they ever expect the sexuality to work when, at best, they are strangers and, at worst, they are enemies?

Many years ago when I (Hal) was working with cancer patients at the Center for the Healing Arts in Los Angeles, a woman came to see me for consultation about a recently diagnosed stomach cancer. She had traveled a considerable distance and was only going to be seeing me for the one visit. She wanted my recommendations. In the course of the interview I asked her whether she drank soft drinks very much. She said that she loved Coke. I asked her how much she drank. Her answer astounded me. She told me that she drank an average of twenty cans of Coke a day. She had done this for about twenty-five years. It never occurred to her that this might not be good. I sat there in shock that she could do this and have no idea that it had anything to do with her stomach cancer.

It is this sense of shock that we often experience when people want to work on their sexual issues. They may have absolutely nothing going for them in their relationship at all, yet sexuality is generally the fall guy that gets blamed for all the woes of the relationship. How often we hear the painful lament: "If only our sexuality was better … then everything would be okay." Our experience is quite the opposite. The *sexuality* is not working because the *relationship* is not working. The trick is to help people unhook from their attachment to the symptom so they can work on the real problem. In a nutshell, the real problem is the totality of communication that is operating between the partners. As the relationship improves, the sexual connection between the partners has a chance to begin to blossom.

THE FOUR REALITIES OF
SEXUALITY AND SENSUALITY

There are four core realities to keep in mind when you consider sexuality in partnership. Read these over now and review them a few times as you read this chapter. Understanding these principles will help you to understand how sexuality is related to the issues of vulnerability and linkage and to the selves in section 1.

First Reality

Sexuality is a particularly sensitive part of relationship. It can engender a combination of vulnerability, feelings of rejection, sexual frustration, and rage that is particularly volatile. Your sense of righteous indignation is usually stronger about sexuality than about any other relational issue. This may be so extreme that the anger and rage can crack the vessel of relationship so that it cannot be repaired.

Second Reality

In most cases the sexual issue is only the tip of the iceberg, no matter how large that tip looks to you or your partner! It becomes the focal point, the lightning rod, for all the other issues that have not been adequately worked out. *You cannot separate your physical relationship from the totality of what happens between you as partners in the other aspects of your life together!*

Third Reality

Sexuality without energetic linkage, or intimacy, is ultimately unsatisfying. For a satisfying sexual relationship, you must learn to recognize when this intimacy is present and when it is not. If it is missing in the partnership, then where has it gone? How are your needs for linkage being satisfied in your life? *Linkage carries the juice of the relationship and when it disappears, there is always something missing in the sexual connection.*

Fourth Reality

The core issue is rarely *what* people are doing wrong sexually but rather *who* it is that is trying to have sex! When you discover the selves that are running the show sexually, the dawn will come, the sun will rise, and things will start to make sense sexually.

ALL YOU EVER WANTED TO KNOW ABOUT SEX: WELL, MAYBE NOT *ALL*

In our work with couples we seldom do direct sexual counseling. For the right people at the right time, direct sexual counseling is important. However, in our experience, we have found that most sexual issues are not based on a sexual problem at all, but are related to what is happening in other parts of the relationship.

Sexual issues can be devastating to a relationship and they can cause the most intense pain and suffering. They often feel catastrophic and insoluble. When partners are in the middle of these tortures they commonly do not want to think about deeper issues. They want the sex to work the way they want it to work, and they want it to work now! The partners think that if they could only get the sex to work properly, then everything would be fine. Of course, the fact that it does not work is generally seen as the problem of the other person.

Men, in particular, often have an interesting response to being denied sexual relations. It may be that the partners have had a good sexual connection for three weeks running. If, on the twenty-second day, the woman does not wish to have sex, the man is devastated. He does not like the feeling of rejection. He often accuses his partner of being frigid, withholding, and thoughtless and he feels as though his world has come to an end. He totally forgets the previous three weeks of good sexual contact! We think this is a fascinating and very specific type of amnesia and we wonder if it is sex linked — perhaps the gene for this is on the male chromosome right next to the one that likes to surf channels rather than watch a single TV program.

Our basic premise: *A comprehensive and satisfying sexuality in partnering does not start and end in the bedroom. That is only one of the places where it lives.* Let's look at some of the ways in which your patterns of relating can affect the sexual connection you have with your partner.

- If you are upset with your partner and feel very judgmental but you say nothing — and this happens often enough in positive bonding patterns — the sexual connection will eventually diminish. Every unspoken reaction becomes a silent judgment. Accumulate enough silent judgments and "Poof" goes the sexuality. If you are upset with your partner and you speak your judgments aloud, letting your judgmental parent do the talking, this, too, is big trouble. We have noticed that this approach is rarely a great sexual turn-on. Sexuality dies pretty quickly when either you or your partner feel like an injured child being victimized by the other's parental attacks. The challenge is to learn how to react to others while we maintain energetic linkage so that the reaction is coming from our aware ego, which has an energetic connection to our partner, rather than from the judgmental parent self, which has no connection.

- If you are never vulnerable in your connection to your partner, you cannot expect the sex to continue to work. If you are always taking care of your partner and feeling responsible for everything, you cannot expect sexuality to maintain its excitement and intensity. If you live as a child in your relationship, giving all your power away to your partner, sexuality can easily die.

- If you live in a relationship without ever expressing any disagreement or negativity, where everything is positive and caring and nurturing and loving, your physical relationship can easily erode. A continuing process of healthy communication is an essential ingredient for a healthy sex life. This includes all kinds of communication, including communication about sexuality, which is frequently the most difficult subject of all. We have often said to couples who are just beginning to seriously and honestly express themselves to each other that *this* is sex, right here and right now. If this works then the physical sex has a chance to work.

• If you are identified with a parenting role and automatically take responsibility for everything, physicality easily dies. If you are run by your inner critic and constantly berate yourself, your body, and your personality for not being right, it's really hard to feel attractive or sexual. If you are addicted to your computer and lovingly caress it until 11 P.M. every night while being totally oblivious of your partner, it is unlikely that your abandoned partner will forever continue to receive you with unbounded enthusiasm.

• If you bury your sensuality because you are living in a monogamous relationship and you are afraid to feel your natural attractions to others (even though you do not act on them), your sexuality and sensuality toward your primary partner will suffer. If you have a five-star pusher running your life and you suddenly slam on the brakes each night to have sex so that you can relax properly and go to sleep, it won't be too long before your partner sees this encounter as somewhat lacking in romance. The list is endless.

What is the basic point of the examples we have just given you? When your physical relationship isn't working, the focus of your attention needs to go toward your relationship in general and not the sexuality in particular. Most of the time the sexuality is a smoke screen that focuses people on the wrong issue. The real question you need to be asking is: "What is wrong with our relationship that throws the sexuality off as badly as it does?"

You need to examine some of the basic issues we dealt with in section 1. Which selves are running your life and your partnership? How does the interaction of these selves affect your communications with your partner? Are you and your partner able to relate to each other's vulnerability so that you can feel safe? Is there real intimacy in your relationship? Do you ever just sit and look at each other, whether in the living room or in the bedroom? These are the kinds of issues that need to be attended to.

SEXUALITY AND SENSUALITY

Most of us are familiar with sexual feelings or energy. The important thing about sexual energy is that it tends to be very focused and very purposive in its function. Sexual energy drives us toward sexual contact and orgasm. As with all of the selves that operate inside of us, sexual energy has a good side and a bad side. The good side is that it feels great and can provide us with much pleasure and release. It also ensures that our species will survive because children are created out of the sexual act.

The down side is the fact that, in its intense focus toward gratification, sexuality by itself is generally not connected to relationship values or to intimacy. In fact, it is often opposed to intimacy. Men have traditionally been trained to be very macho when it comes to sexuality and to value sexuality rather than intimacy. Much of men's sense of self worth rests around the issue of "being successful" sexually with partners rather than the quality of their relationship with them.

Intimacy exists on four levels: physical, emotional, psychological, and spiritual. Each of these has the possibility of an energetic expression. Without emotional, psychological, and spiritual intimacy a sexual relationship is just what it appears to be, purely physical. In their younger years this generally works for people because they usually don't know any better and it feels good. As they get older, many people require a deeper and more total connection to their partner. What we want to focus on here is the issue of *physical intimacy*. What is missing for most people is the experience of a sensuality or physical intimacy independent of sexuality. Because of our fondness for mythological parallels, we have named this kind of sensual energy the *Aphrodite energy*.

Although Aphrodite was a female goddess in Greek mythology, as a self or energy living inside of us it belongs as much to men as it does to women. In our experience women seem to have a more natural connection to intimacy in general, and to physical intimacy, in particular than men. The lines have been blurring in recent times, however, as more women enter the workplace and more men begin to embrace the need for intimate relationships.

Aphrodite energy is very different from a sexual response. The origin of the feeling is not located specifically in the sexual area. You can feel it throughout your whole body. It is like a subtle vibration in the skin. When you feel it, you feel alive. When it is present, it can provide an easy bridge to sexuality but it can also exist by itself. It is a very beautiful and a very empowering kind of energy to have available. It feels as though your whole body is buzzing.

This energy gives us the feeling of being alive and in our bodies. All sensory experience is heightened. The sun looks brighter and the grass is greener. The sense of touch is very much sensitized and intensified. Sounds are amplified and smells are enhanced. It is not simply a quantitative change in sensory experience. It is an actual qualitative change.

This Aphrodite energy may be present during a sexual connection, although more often it is not. You may yearn for it not knowing what it is that calls to you. This kind of connection, this sensuality, is usually present after the orgasm as well as before it. It is difficult to cultivate Aphrodite energy if you are very driven, very mental, very self-critical, very perfectionistic, or any combination of these. This kind of energy requires a softer and somewhat slower drummer to beat the rhythm of your life.

To help you experience this sensual energy, we designed a series of exercises. Please follow them only if they seem appropriate to you. Feel free to stop at any point if they are not working for you or your partner. Stop if, you feel like stopping at any point for whatever reason, including no reason at all.

There is no physical contact in any of these exercises. To do them, set aside at least a half hour during which you can work with your partner in a private space without being interrupted. Try not to think very much, just relax. This will allow you to concentrate on the subtleties of the energetic interactions. Comfort is all-important, so wear comfortable clothes and, preferably, no shoes. These exercises should also be done indoors away from any distracting breezes or sounds. We recommend that you keep your eyes open during these exercises.

SENSUALITY EXERCISE 1
Partners A and B Exchange Sensual Energy

For this exercise you and your partner should be sitting comfortably, facing each other about two to three feet apart. Designate one of you as Partner A and the other as Partner B.

In this exercise you will learn how to access sensual rather than sexual energies. As we have mentioned before, the sensual energies are located in the skin of the whole body and are felt as a subtle vibration.

1. Face each other and allow the energy to build between you. Keep your sexual energies closed as best you can. You can do this by imagining that you are pulling the energy of the pelvis away from your partner or you can imagine a door that you close over the pelvic area.

2. As you sit with each other, you will soon begin to feel a gentle buzzing in your skin. You may want to visualize an

Aphrodite image if you are so inclined. In mythology she is a goddess of love and sensuality. Just picture her in your imagination and imagine that her energy is available to you. Allow this energy to build between the two of you.

3. Once you are experiencing this sensual buzz, decide together when to turn it down.

4. After you have turned it down, wait for thirty seconds or more and then turn it up again. Practice turning the energies up and down several different times. What you are ultimately trying to learn is how to become aware of the different energies and then how to use them instead of them using you.

5. Repeat this exercise two or three times.

SENSUALITY EXERCISE 2
Partner A Sends Sensual Energy

In this exercise, Partner A turns on the sensuality and Partner B is the passive receiver. Partner B experiences the sending of Partner A's energy and then reports back to A and tries to help A learn how to use this energy.

1. Facing each other again, Partner A turns on the Aphrodite energy. After B acknowledges the feeling of the sensuality, A will now turn down the sensual energy, keep it down for about thirty seconds, and then open it again and repeat the procedure two or three times. Take time to share what is happening with your partner. Decide together how many times you would like to repeat this.

Please remember that with sensual energy the focus is not on the lower pelvic area, where sexual energy is concentrated. This full-bodied buzz really has to do with our sensual response to *all* of life, and is more than just sexual.

SENSUALITY EXERCISE 3
Partner B Sends Sensual Energy

Repeat the previous exercise, but reverse partners. In this exercise, Partner B turns on the sensuality and Partner A is the passive receiver. Partner A experiences the sending of Partner B's energy and then reports back to B and tries to help B learn how to use this energy.

SENSUALITY EXERCISE 4
Personal and Impersonal Aphrodite Energies

This is the final exercise of the sensuality series and a very important one. In these exercises, you are learning how to become aware of the Aphrodite energy and, furthermore, how to use it with your partner. In using this energy in the world, however, it is really helpful to know the difference between personal and impersonal Aphrodite energies and how to use them.

In chapter 5 on linkage and energetic connection, you learned how to recognize personal and impersonal energy. We all need both of these in our partnering, and many relationships founder on the issue of how these are used by each partner. In this exercise you will use your knowledge of personal and impersonal energy and apply it to Aphrodite energy.

We do not believe it is a good idea to go through the world with one's personal Aphrodite showing all the time. When Aphrodite energy comes through the personal side it has no boundaries; this makes it very difficult for us to establish proper boundaries because our energetic space is constantly vulnerable to being invaded. You need to make careful choices about the use of the personal Aphrodite.

On the other hand, you can use the impersonal Aphrodite and have her available full time. She has boundaries and isn't constantly pulling in attentive and remarkably persistent admirers. It is much easier for us to learn to handle ourselves with this impersonal Aphrodite present. She brings us the gift of sensual energy but, at the same time, she allows us to have boundaries.

1. *Personal energy.* In this exercise Partners A and B both bring in personal energy. If you are sensitive you will actually feel what we refer to as the energy field or linkage between you. Remember, too, that you can control this personal energy and make it more or less personal by using an imaginary valve or control system to turn the energy up or down.

2. *Personal Aphrodite.* Once you have established a personal energy linkage you may now bring in the Aphrodite or sensuality energy. See what this feels like. With personal Aphrodite energy you are actually embracing your partner with your energy field.

3. *Impersonal Aphrodite.* After a minute or so, begin to imagine simply withdrawing your energy from your partner. As you do this, you will be moving to a more impersonal place. See what Aphrodite feels like and looks like from this place. To get a clear picture of what this is like, think of a good cocktail waitress who has a perfect blend of impersonal and personal Aphrodite energy. Her message is clear: "Look and enjoy but don't touch!"

It is relatively easy to train people in the energetics of relationship when we are physically together with them. We have successfully taught couples, small groups, and very large groups. Teaching these skills in a book is much more difficult. So we ask you to be patient with yourselves as you go through these exercises. Take your time and try them more than once. When partners begin to experience the Aphrodite energy with each other on a regular basis a whole new dimension is added to their connection and all the hard work will be seen as quite worth worthwhile.

A COMPOSITE EXAMPLE OF A "SEXUAL PROBLEM"

This chapter is about sexuality and sensuality, but really we are not talking about sexuality and "how to do it properly" because we personally do not know how to "do it properly." People are too different and their needs are too different. Sexuality training or counseling can be effective for the right person at the right place and the right time. We leave it to you to determine if such counseling is appropriate for you and to make your own choices.

The primary sexual training that we do is oriented toward helping people in general, and couples in particular, to learn how to be together on a physical, emotional, mental, spiritual, and energetic level with real choice available to them. This, of course, means that they must learn to differentiate sensuality from sexuality as we have done in the prior exercises.

Through the years we have learned that the vast majority of sexual problems are relational in origin. Even when a sexual issue pre-exists in the relationship, a true partnering attitude gives you the chance to work out the emotional issues that were present before the partners got together.

Here we will present a composite example of a sexual problem that incorporates many of the problems we see so commonly in our work. Marvin is a forty-two-year-old businessman who is very extroverted, very successful, and very driven. For Marvin his work is first and his children are second. Third in priority is watching television to help him unwind and fourth is trying to take care of himself physically since he fears a heart attack may be imminent. He has no access to his own feelings of vulnerability. The only way it comes out is in his fear of a heart attack. Last in the priority sweepstakes is his thirty-six-year-old wife, Lois. Marvin does not deliberately set out to make her last. This is just the way it has developed over the years.

Marvin and Lois have been together for fifteen years. She is very much his polar opposite in many ways. She is much quieter, enjoys herself at home very much, and in general operates out of a much slower energy. She is very sensitive and vulnerable and spends a great deal of time with their two children. In the early years of the relationship, things worked very well on a sexual level. The sexuality began to erode seriously after the birth of their first child, a remarkably common happening.

In the initial interview Marvin complains that Lois never wants sex and never initiates sex. He also complains that when they have sexual relations she does it out of duty and they would be better off if there were no sex at all. He feels she is a very good mother but blames her for not having any time because she spends it on household things. Sometimes when they go out of town things are better but it never lasts. He has no other complaints about her and doesn't feel negative toward her in any other area but the sexual one. He doesn't like negativity in the home and tries to stay away from it. As a matter of fact, he is unhappy about how bitter and angry he has become because of this sexual issue.

Marvin doesn't want to have an affair, though he has been thinking about it and feels that if the sexual thing isn't solved the marriage will go under. He has become increasingly negative and feels as though he is constantly irritable and judgmental. He blames everything on the lack of sex in the relationship. He also feels that Lois has become increasingly judgmental toward him and he says that getting into bed with her at night feels like stepping into a deep freeze. The issue has reached nightmare proportions.

Lois also feels that the deterioration in the relationship began with the birth of their first child, though she is aware that things were becoming negative earlier than that. She feels particularly close to the firstborn, a son, and Marvin has become equally close to the second child, a daughter. She says that Marvin is too driven: "He never stops! It's just go and go and go and go." It exhausts her and she doesn't feel the same attraction to him any longer. "His drive for money and success is too great and he's totally controlling about finances. He claims he's very generous, but in fact I'm on an allowance and even though I can spend what I want, all the money is ultimately controlled by him. I don't even know how much money we have. He freaks out whenever I ask any questions in this area."

Lois has other observations as well. She is a people-oriented person and she has given a great deal of thought to their relationship. She adds: "Marvin never sits still. We can never just be quiet with each other. He never holds me. He never touches me. Sex for him is going to bed and having intercourse. There is no intimacy between us, not physical and not emotional. He's always judging me and I'm feeling like a professional victim. He's drinking more than I like though he denies that there is a problem. I don't generally react to him about things I don't like. We've never done that. Neither of us likes arguments or negative feelings, but the sexuality now is poisoning everything and I'm sitting in judgment toward him all the time."

We could go on with this list of grievances for a very long time, particularly because we are using Marvin and Lois as a composite couple and they represent a wide range of common conflicts. They recognize that the marriage is in trouble, but the whole focus of their concern and understanding remains on the sexual sphere. Let's first consider the four points of our core reality system as we look at their life together.

First, they are both locked in a death embrace of righteous judgment with each other. This is accelerating and soon the relationship vessel will crack completely. Second, they see only the tip of the iceberg and for them the only real problem is the sexual problem. Marvin even says that nothing else bothers him. If the sex worked then he would be a happy man. How often we have heard that statement in the course of our work with couples. Third, they have not a notion that their everyday interactions have anything to do with their sexual issue. There is no intimacy, no energetic linkage between them and there has not been for some time.

Finally, there are the selves. Which selves in Marvin are seeking sexual contact with Lois? There is a very needy child who is never taken care of except through sex, food, and alcohol. There is an angry, righteous father-judge-patriarch who demands what is coming to him and who sees Lois as failing in her duty as a woman. Not a very romantic or appealing group.

Which selves are operating in Lois? There is the compliant daughter who occasionally does her duty because she recognizes that men do need sex and it has to be provided for them periodically. As the anger has built up in the relationship, there is a victim daughter who feels she is being abused. Accompanying this victim daughter is a very righteous and judgmental mother who is enraged and wishes that Marvin would leave the house, or die, or just get out of her face. Not a very sensual, loving, or welcoming group.

What is the work then that Marvin and Lois need to do? How can they begin to work out of the mess they are in? The answer to this question is the same whether the symptom is a sexual one or not. We each have to work with our relationship as a whole system of interactions and choices.

They have taken the first step by seeking help. In doing so, they have begun to break the cycle of abuse that has taken over their interactions. Not all relationships deteriorate to this level, of course, but the principles are the same. Asking for help is a big step because so many people still feel ashamed of seeking counseling.

To begin with, Marvin and Lois must learn how to share with each other some of the nonsexual things that bother them in the relationship. Until they learn that there is a gigantic iceberg under the surface of the water, they will stay forever trapped at the level of the symptom.

There are many different ways to do this, but the most traditional would be to have Lois tell Marvin what he does that bothers her. Marvin is asked to remain silent during this time. He is not expected to respond to Lois, just to listen and to try to hear what she is saying. After she is finished, it is Marvin's turn to do the same thing and Lois is silent. After this is finished, they repeat the procedure but this time expressing the positive feelings, first one and then the other. If the level of anger in a relationship is too high, starting with this procedure is not advisable. Other work is necessary before this kind of sharing can be done.

Here is a summary of what Lois said to Marvin over a period of several sessions with our support and encouragement: "I wish you would slow down. You behave like a racing car out of control. Having sex with you is like having a race car driver stop in for servicing. I wish you would put the toilet seat down when you're through with it. It isn't fun at night to sit down and fall into the toilet. I wish you would once, just once, offer to help around the house. I know that you are always telling me to get more help, but couldn't you just once return a cup to the sink and wash it. I hate when you get the toothpaste all over the sink. Sometimes I think that I have three children instead of two. I hate when we are in a restaurant and you stare at other women like an adolescent in heat. Sometimes I just wish you would have an affair and get it over with. And I wish you would stop talking about our personal life when we are out socially. I'm very shy and I don't like being made public that way."

Once one of the partners gets going in this process, it is quite remarkable to observe the multiplicity of issues that are troublesome and that have never been dealt with. Imagine the effect that holding in all of these unspoken reactions and the accumulating judgment can have over many years' time. How could Lois possibly, for this reason alone, maintain a sexual response? Sometimes both partners close down sexually, but more often one partner closes down sexually and the other becomes more sexually demanding.

Marvin, over time, is able to begin to express his own litany of complaints. The challenge with him was helping him to talk about trouble spots other than those in the sexual arena. Here is a summary of some of the issues Marvin had with Lois: "I married a woman and got a mother. From the time that Ralph (the son) was born you changed completely. You're not married to me. You're married to this house and to your chores and to your friends. You spend hours talking to your friends. You complain that I don't touch you but if I do reach out you find an excuse to get away. You don't like the bathroom when I get it dirty and I can't stand your compulsive cleanliness. God forbid a cup should be left out or anything should be out of place."

Now we are beginning to deal with what is underneath the tip of the iceberg. Essentially, Marvin and Lois have to do the work that we all have to do in relationship. Why do you think it is that well over half of all marriages end in divorce and a large percentage of the remaining marriages are considered inadequate by their partners? This is not some deep esoteric secret. This is not because marriage is cursed and love is cursed once you get married. *Marriages break up primarily because the couple never become partners. They never commit themselves to work on themselves and on the relationship itself.* They often don't know how.

Fortunately, today we have an ever-increasing number of therapists who work with couples and relationship books that help point the way. From our perspective, Marvin and Lois must learn about their primary and disowned selves. Marvin and Lois are opposites of each other. Because of this, they can be teachers for each other once they begin to separate from the inner selves that are running their lives. They must learn that the things they can't stand about each other are in fact a part of their disowned self system.

Underneath all of the anger and judgment that flies between Marvin and Lois lies their vulnerability. Neither of them has ever learned how to be vulnerable in a relationship, how to communicate feelings of fear and shyness and anxiety and loneliness. When vulnerability is disowned, power steps in to fill the void and power can become very raw and very cruel. Marvin and Lois will have to learn how to feel and then to communicate their vulnerability to one another.

THE GIFT IN SEXUAL CHALLENGES

When we are being crucified by the problems of life it is diffi-cult to look at the potential blessings and possibilities that lie at the other end of the dark tunnel we are traversing. It is usually either deep psychic pain or a serious illness or some combination of both factors that drives most of us to start the journey of personal trans-formation. A very difficult sexual relationship often becomes the ultimate pain point that forces a person to seek help and take the journey of personal growth.

This is a very different way of thinking about physical discom-fort or actual illness. You can look at it as a curse, something to be eliminated. You can also look at illness as a teacher, something you can learn from so that you can determine what is out of balance in your life. So it is with all of life's pain. You can choose the surgical method and try to eradicate the pain and the symptom or you can ask yourself, "What is the teaching in this pain? What is the teach-ing in this relationship? What must I do to learn what I must learn?"

Marvin is a driven man. Because of his intense suffering he is forced to seek help. He has a chance to separate from a murder-ous pusher energy that has driven him all his life and that will most likely create an early heart attack. He has a chance to learn about his vulnerability and dramatically change the quality of his rela-tionships at home and away from home.

Lois has been a homebody who is afraid to step out into the world. As she realizes this she has more choices available to her; she may even decide to go to work or to school or to do something in the world that is calling out to her. She has a chance to see that her sexuality and sensuality have died and that her primary linkage part-ner is her son rather than her husband. This does not do the son any favors, and he will get freed and be able to live his own life more fully as Lois begins to understand her need for linkage and begins to move her energetic linkage to Marvin. For both Marvin and Lois, the trans-formation of their relationship into a partnering process would give each of them the chance to learn from, respect, and love the other.

SEXUALITY AND POSITIVE BONDING PATTERNS

We have just shown you how sexual difficulties can be just one symptom of a very negative bonding pattern. But, what about positive bonding patterns in which the good child self of one partner bonds with the loving, responsible parent of the other (and vice versa) and everything is sweet, reasonable, loving, and caring?

These bonding patterns usually stifle sexuality by forcing us into our "best" and most proper behavior. We pretend that we are not sexual beings. We try not to let our partners know if we are attracted elsewhere. As a matter of fact, we try not to let ourselves know. We do our best to stifle any sensual or sexual impulses that arise outside of the primary relationship.

But, as we like to say, Aphrodite (the goddess of love and sensuality) is a proud and demanding goddess. She will not allow us to chain her to the conjugal bed. She is either present in all parts of our lives — and this means that we feel all our sexual attractions even though we do not necessarily act upon them — or she is not present in any. So if we ignore her in life and try to bring her into the bedroom, she often eludes us.

This again brings us to the challenge of standing between opposites. This time the opposites are our monogamous selves that want to preserve an exclusive sexuality and our non-monogamous selves that feel sexual attractions and would prefer to roam. Balancing these two requires the aware ego that we talked about, the one that stands on two legs and can make a conscious commitment to monogamy and feel our sexual urges. The reward for doing this is an enhanced sexuality and sensuality in our partnering.

There are some partners who live in a positive bonding pattern and have very active and apparently satisfactory sex lives. They may have arguments or get into negative bonding patterns from time to time, but basically the sexual area seems fine.

It is interesting to see which selves are involved in these couples' sexual connections. Very often it is the same selves that are in the positive bonding pattern and that run the rest of the relationship. The pleaser is always happy to grant a partner's sexual wishes. The responsible mother will see to it that her partner is completely satisfied and she will even know the frequency of sexual contact that is necessary. Even a pusher will take into consideration that sexuality is an important part of relationship and will see to it that the sexual area is not neglected. Many men take care of their vulnerability and satisfy their needs for emotional contact and nurturing by making sexual contact with their partners.

HEALING MARVIN AND LOIS: WHAT NEEDS TO BE DONE

Marvin and Lois have been very kind to us. The least we can do is point them in the right direction so that they can begin to move out of the dangerous jungle they are currently living in. They can learn to do the following things by talking together, by reading books and sharing ideas, by attending workshops and classes on relationship, or by consulting with a therapist who works with couples. They also might want to read section 1 of this book and see how their relationship fits in. Now let's give them some other ideas.

• Marvin and Lois must begin to recognize that they are teachers for each other and that each is carrying selves that the other person is missing. The universe arranges relationship with mathematical precision. Marvin needs the introversion, quietness, vulnerability, and general intimacy and softer sexuality that Lois carries for him. Lois needs some of the extroversion, dynamic drive, intense sexuality, and business and financial experience that Marvin carries for her.

• They need to suspend hostilities over sexuality for a period of time. They must recognize that a deteriorating sex life is only a symptom of a relationship that has gone sour. It can't be sweetened until they put down the clubs they are using so far as the sexual difficulties are concerned.

• They might begin to spend some regular time reading books on relationship together, or attending workshops or classes together. There is much to learn. They can start taking advantage of what is out there. In addition to our own books and tapes, in the back of this book we have listed a number of other books on relationship that we feel would be helpful to you as well as to Lois and Marvin.

• They must each discover their own primary and disowned selves and learn that their judgments toward one another are a reflection of these disowned selves.

• They must learn which selves are operating between them in their relationship. Lois is afraid of being out in the world. This automatically puts her husband into a father role with her. Marvin is cut off from his vulnerability. This means that Lois is responsible for taking care of his vulnerability, a job that ultimately she will resent.

• Both must learn how to feel and communicate their vulnerability.

• Both must begin a process of honest communication with each other and if it takes outside help to do this, so be it. This includes learning to communicate without judgment or demands about their sexual feelings, needs, and preferences in energetic linkage.

• They need to begin to experience linkage. They need to spend time just sitting and being with each other. It is their linkage that provides the real sense of intimacy and the feeling of being fed by each other.

- They must both learn how they have linked to their children and how this too special connection to the children has been a factor in their separation from each other. They must learn how to continue to give to their children, but to maintain for themselves the special linkage that is theirs alone.

These nine points represent the start of the journey of redemption. We have seen such relationships change for the better many, many times as people began to do this work. If a relationship must end, so be it. However, we hate to see relationships end for the wrong reason, which for us is not doing the basic work that we are all capable of doing.

PRACTICAL IDEAS FOR ENHANCING SEXUALITY

We would like to make some practical suggestions about things you can do to enhance and support the sensuality and sexuality of your relationship. Please remember, these are *only* feasible once the communication process is working and some level of linkage can be maintained.

Making a Date — A Special Time for Sexual Contact

It is difficult to make love while driving on the freeway. It is also difficult to have a proper sexual connection if you have been driving on the psychological freeway of life for many hours and then suddenly veer off into your bedroom in order to have sex. This may work early in a relationship but for real partners, a much more intimate setting is necessary.

More practically, if one partner is working at the computer or responsibly taking care of friends and family until bedtime and then goes into the bedroom to meet the other partner, there is no sense of intimacy or continuity of connection. One minute they are apart and the next moment the partners are together and ready to be sexual. We are not insisting that every sexual encounter must be a deep communion. That can also become a chore. We do suggest, however, that as time passes, your sexual encounters must begin to touch your deeper intimacy needs or the sexuality will founder. Actually, even at the beginning of a relationship, the feeling of connection and intimacy is a particularly delicious addition to sexuality.

The moral to the story is that you must be conscious in the planning of at least some of your sexual encounters. Jack Zimmerman, Ph.D., and Jaquelyn McCandless, M.D., in their book *Flesh and Spirit,* recommend scheduling regular times for coming together. This works for many couples but not for all. There are several advantages to this planning. The first is apparent for couples where there is a strong inequality in sexual needs. This gives the partner who worries about not having enough sex the reassurance that there are scheduled times that can be counted on. On the other side, for the partner who has less of a sexual drive and has felt bombarded by a constant demand for sexual contact, there is the freedom of knowing that there are some boundaries on the sexuality. So, each one's needs are spoken, honored, and met.

Perhaps the greatest advantage of this plan is that when you know that you are going to come together on Wednesday evening, you treat it like a "date" and prepare for it. You do not stay at your computer until 8:59:59 P.M. and then race into the bedroom. Preparation means getting the room ready, lighting candles, incense, or whatever is appropriate to the partners' taste in the matter. Preparation means ritualizing some of the sexual contact so that it is not just relaxation by orgasm each time you come together.

If you share any kind of spiritual outlook, creating time and space around and within the sexuality for spiritual ritual can be very meaningful. It is possible to meditate together, to simply sit and exchange energy for a period of time, to pray together, and to visualize together. McCandless and Zimmerman speak of invoking "the third," which is the spiritual dimension. This takes time. The payoff is a much deeper sense of connection to each other during the sexual act.

From our perspective, one of the most important things we can do is to learn to create an energetic connection before we begin to make love. The longer partners are together the more important this becomes.

Linkage During Sexuality

Creating an energetic linkage during lovemaking is important. Do you look at your partner when you make love? Do you make contact in other ways? If you don't, the sexual act can become a turning inward that has nothing to do with your partner. When this happens one of the partners usually becomes sensitive to it and brings it up as a problem. So take some time to just *be* with one another, to focus on each other and your connection. Don't rush.

It is possible to work on the issue of energetic linkage during the process of lovemaking. You can use the linkage exercises in chapter 5 or the sensuality exercises in this chapter to familiarize yourself with energetic linkage. You might even develop your own variation of these as a warm-up for lovemaking. Linkage during lovemaking feels really good. However, this is *not* a substitute for linkage when you are not together in a sexual way. Otherwise the only linkage in your relationship may occur during the physical connection and ultimately this can be a problem.

Time Away from the Home

The home in which you live with your partner and children becomes a place of duty, responsibility, and habitual patterns of behavior. We say that it is the dwelling place of the primary selves. It is usually not very conducive to an intimate sexual or sensual connection.

We recommend very strongly to partners that they get away from the house *alone* (no children, no work) once a month if possible and once every six weeks at a minimum. It is best for this to be at least an overnight. We also recommend that other times are built into the week when the partners are alone and without children. In order to maintain sexual intimacy in partnering we need to spend quality time as partners, totally separate from our relationship to each other in the family setting.

Couples often will say that they can't afford to go away like this and that they can't afford the cost of baby-sitters. There are many ways around this. You can arrange with friends to have "child swapping" clubs where you take turns taking care of each others' children. This can be done for an afternoon, for an evening, or for a weekend so that you have your own house to yourself. It is essential that we not make children into our jailers.

If you do not fight to preserve quality time for yourselves, the intimacy of the relationship will erode and you will wake up one morning wondering how you managed to be living with someone that you love like a sister or a brother rather than as a romantic partner. Sex does not work in this kind of relationship.

This is not always easy to do. There are millions of reasons why there is no time and no money available. But, we might point out, there are many ways to arrange for this if you give it the priority it deserves. It is always amazing to us to observe how much entitlement children have and how little their parents have with the family. Parents often don't feel entitled to spend time alone with one another because it seems self-indulgent. We pay a big price when the partnership's linkage and intimacy break down. Unhappy partners do not make for happy and capable parents, and children were not meant to become our primary partners. We need to have the mentality of a sage and the power of a warrior to be able to fight for partnering and do whatever is necessary to make it work and work well!

Basically, dealing with sexual issues is no different than dealing with any other kind of issue in relationship. It is just more painful and potentially more explosive. Whatever the problems are, we have to do the work that leads to true partnering. Whether these problems are sexual or nonsexual, they are all opportunities for deep learning.

Chapter 7

PARTNERING AS A BUSINESS VENTURE: LEARNING TO SHARE THE DETAILS OF LIFE

If you want a relationship that is intimate and fulfilling, where being together feeds you like a full and delicious meal, where a soul reality is a part of your ongoing interactions, then you must work together to create the space and time your relationship needs. These business meetings give you a way to deal with the overwhelming details of modern life as true partners.

Life is immensely complicated. We are besieged with details and responsibilities, with things we must do and things we ought to do. In our age of technology, there are new challenges as we work to gain some kind of mastery over the latest electronic helpers, computers, faxes, electronic mail, software programs, and ever more complex telecommunications equipment.

We have our jobs, our autos, our cell phones, our friends, our family, our physical condition, our education, our written calendars, and our electronic calendars. Now we have added to all this the need for personal growth. The list is endless and so far we have only been talking about a single individual. The complexity increases as we enter into partnership. Indeed, that might not even be the end of it. The partnership might include a larger family system. We are indeed running a business, each of us, whether alone or in partnership. *Our observation of couples through the years has shown that very few people seem to recognize the complexity of the business they are running.* It is truly a joint venture. In most cases of personal relationship, however, people refuse to think of partnering in a business sense at all. It seems a bit too unromantic.

This concept of joint venture in relationship is a relatively new idea. Decision making in couples has largely been done via the roles (or primary selves) that partners played out with each other. For example, the wife's traditional role is to take care of the home and the husband's traditional role is to earn the money. This forces them into specific behaviors. The wife cooks the food, washes the dishes, and takes care of the children. Her life in the world outside the home is quite limited. Her picture of herself is governed by this role. The traditional male in this scheme becomes the breadwinner. He works hard and when he comes home, he enters his wife's domain. The actual form of these patterns of behavior will vary from couple to couple. What is clear is that these ways of relating become imbedded in concrete and after a while the family system is quite rigid.

A joint business venture in personal relationships is different. It means that there is equality between the partners. *Everything* — we repeat — *everything* needs to be dealt with by *both* partners. If partners do not find a regular way to deal with this business–decision making aspect of relationship, joint business decisions are never made. Instead, each partner reverts to the default position.

What do we mean by the default position in relationship? In computer terminology, the default position is a set position that occurs automatically unless something is changed to make it come up in a different way. For instance, your default position in print type is Helvetica. This means that the Helvetica font (or type of print) comes up automatically; this is the font that was originally programmed into your computer and it is the font you will get unless you decide to change it. Changing the font requires choice and action. You are free to examine and then choose among dozens of possible fonts. Now you can make a final decision based on your needs for the present time rather than be limited to the original programming. At another time, when you tire of the new font, you might choose something totally different.

The default position is a beautiful analogy to primary selves. Let's say that there is dry cleaning that needs to be picked up. The dry cleaner is open Monday through Saturday. The husband is at work and the wife is home with the children. Classically, the default position would be that the wife picks up the cleaning. After all, she is at home and her husband is at work earning the money. She can pick up the cleaning on her way to, or from, dropping off the children at school or driving them to their music lessons in the afternoon. No real decision is made about this by either of them. They have fallen into their traditional stereotypical roles — the default position — and it all feels very natural and proper. It makes perfect sense because this is how the relationship has always been. This is not partnering. This is living the relationship out of set roles or primary selves that were programmed into our psychic systems early in life. We can assure you that living out these roles in this automatic fashion will eventually destroy the vitality of the relationship.

In a joint venture partnership, you decide how you will share the responsibilities. Maybe the dry cleaner is right next to the kids' school, and Partner A picks up the dry cleaning the majority of the time. And maybe Partner B has a market next to the office, and so it is Partner B's responsibility to do the marketing. You can also split some of the tasks or errands that need to be accomplished during the day, but remember to remain flexible. That is, if Partner A simply can't get to the dry cleaner due to conflicting appointments, then Partner B shifts his or her schedule around to pick up the dry cleaning that week.

The same kinds of choices need to be made for the most mundane of tasks. How is the marketing going to get done? How are we going to arrange for the car to be washed? How about taking the kids to the doctor or the dog to the vet? All chores, tasks, and responsibilities — even the more traditional male-oriented respon-sibilities such as managing the family's finances — are shared between the two parties. The issue here isn't which partner does it. The issue is that a conscious choice must be made between the partners so that actions do not come from the default (primary self) position.

THE BUSINESS MEETING

To bring real choice and a new flexibility and life to relationship, we recommend to partners that they schedule regular business meetings with each other. Why do so many people resist this idea? They feel that business meetings are too cold and impersonal, that they belong to a real business but not to a relationship. These part-ners want their relationship to be more personal and intimate. They say that they want their relationship to be spontaneous and not run like a business. They add that they are afraid this will take the romance out of their relationship.

The reality is that if you do not take care of the business side of a relationship you can kiss the romance good-bye. There is just too much to take care of these days, and partners must build into their relationship a way of handling all these details of life.

We recommend a minimum of one meeting a week and possi-bly two or three. More frequent meetings generally mean shorter meetings and they have the advantage of allowing partners to stay on top of things more effectively. Each partner prepares an agenda for the business meeting and *everything* — we repeat — *everything* goes on this agenda.

What kinds of things might be on the agenda?

• You have each made a number of appointments since the last meeting. You need to coordinate and update your schedules.

- Who is going to return the various phone calls?
- Who is going to pick up the dry cleaning?
- Who is going to review your insurance policy?
- There are three social invitations. Which will you accept and which will you reject?
- The upstairs toilet is still having problems. Should a new toilet be considered?
- Intimacy time: What times during the week are you spending together without the children? What evenings do you have set aside for each other? Possibly Partner B proposes a lunch or a breakfast out one day.
- Family matters: Partner A's mother has called to invite the family for the holidays that are six months away. What do you want to do about this?
- Grievances: Partner A has some personal grievances that need to be expressed. This can be dealt with now or it can be dealt with at a separate time to be planned now. It is very nice to have fantasies about being spontaneous in your reactions to each other in a partnership. The reality is that when you don't make time for personal sharing it generally doesn't happen and the relationship functions increasingly in a positive bond pattern.
- There is a meeting at school for one of the children. Who will be attending this?
- Partner B is confused about the finances and wants to know what is going on.
- The partners have decided to keep separate bank accounts and contribute to a joint third account. Who takes care of reconciling the monthly statements and makes sure things are okay?
- The house needs cleaning. Who is going to clean it or make arrangements for a cleaner?
- Who is going to do the cooking and cleanup on the different nights?

• Partner B wants a new car. Possibly the house needs painting. Both partners want a new deck.

• Partner A wants a lock put on the bedroom door. How does Partner B feel about this and how is this going to be done?

• What about this year's vacation?

• Investment matters: You need to make decisions on how to invest your savings. If you decide that Partner A will be in charge of this, then that is the choice you make for now. It may change later. However, Partner A does not work entirely alone, but must report back to Partner B as scheduled. Otherwise Partner B abdicates all responsibility for the investments and this can cause a great deal of trouble later on. You may wish to schedule a separate meeting for investments because you need more research. If so, who will do the research?

This list of possibilities is meant to give you a feeling about the kinds of things that need discussion. Most business meetings will be covering only a few points. We have found that it is important to deal with these details on a regular basis or else they infiltrate everything that partners do together and they take over the relationship. The times that are supposedly devoted to intimacy get filled up with discussions of a multitude of extraneous concerns because they all demand action, or at least a game plan. Worse than using intimacy time to talk about them is the tendency to allow these issues to simply invade our minds until we can never stop thinking about them, no matter what the circumstances. These thoughts have even been known to invade our sexual activities.

RESTING INTO VERSUS ABDICATION

One of the great advantages of a partnership is that each partner has a chance to rest into the other and neither one has to be an expert in everything. We like the expression "to rest into" because it gives such a graphic picture of this particular way of partnering. You do not lean on your partner, you do not become dependent upon your partner, you just rest into your partner's special strengths.

For example, in our relationship Sidra handles the finances. She keeps her own records on our personal finances and she supervises the business finances that are handled through our professional office. Hal rests into her in this area because she is very gifted with finances and he feels very protected and safe with her in charge. On the other hand, Hal handles the professional inquiries regarding trainings, private work, and lectures and Sidra rests into him coordinating the schedule because he is very comfortable in this area and does it well.

At business meetings, however, Hal reports to Sidra and Sidra reports to Hal so that both are made aware of what has been happening and each has a chance to okay what the other has been doing. If either of us is left out of the information loop on the other's activities there is a potential for trouble. If an investment goes sour and Hal didn't pay attention to it, then he can easily go into his negative father self and start to judge Sidra. Conversely, if a program is planned without Sidra seriously considering whether or not she really wants to do it, then when the program time arrives and she doesn't feel like teaching at that time, she can easily go into judgment toward Hal and they are in trouble. When you rest into a partner consciously, real choices are still being made.

Whenever we totally surrender responsibility in any area of life to someone else, we become a child to the other person and there is an automatic parent-child bonding pattern. Whenever we accept total responsibility for any area in a relationship, we assume the role of parent and automatically enter into the parental side of the bonding pattern in this area. Bonding patterns destroy intimacy and a lack of intimacy erodes the quality of sexuality, so the stakes are high.

FINANCES

It is essential for partners to be as clear as possible about the handling of money. Many of the issues that come up in business meetings are in relationship to finances. What usually makes these discussions difficult is that the partners have very different primary selves when it comes to money. This is why the concepts of the many selves and bonding patterns discussed in chapters 2 and 3 are so important to understand. It is very helpful to know who it is in you that is talking with your partner about the finances.

It is amazing to us that many women know nothing about business and finance and, what is more astounding, do not care to learn anything about it. It is very common for a woman client to tell us that she knows nothing about the financial dealings of her husband! She says that her husband gives her as much money as she needs and that is good enough for her.

The problem is that this locks the woman into the role of daughter so far as the financial world is concerned. If she is lucky, when her husband dies his affairs may be in order. However, many times the husband's affairs are not in order and the wife has little or no money after his death. Life is not kind to those of us who insist upon remaining sons and daughters to our partners, especially when it comes to the world of business and finance.

This abdication of power has its roots in centuries of patriarchal training and it is only in recent history that women have begun to step out of their assigned roles. It is important to note that this kind of stereotypical behavior is equally true in same-sex partnering where one member of the couple is generally identified with a more patriarchal role so far as money is concerned. In partnering, constant clarification needs to take place in regard to money because the stakes are so high and the power issues are so great. What is it then that needs to happen on a financial-business level to assure that a couple functions in a partnership rather than in a parent-child mode?

When partners first come together, they must make clear agreements about what is going to happen to the existing monies they each bring with them. Then they must decide what will be done with the income that will be created in the future by each partner. Partners have a choice of combining their money or keeping their money separate and creating a joint account for joint expenses. They must be clear with each other not just about what they plan to do but also about how they feel. In an ordinary relationship, people do what they want. In a partnership, the partners are always working through joint agreement.

Let us say that Carlos is a man of some wealth and he marries Maria, a woman of lesser wealth. He wants to buy a new expensive car. He has earned this money and has plenty of it. He may well ask why he should hesitate buying anything when he made the money and he can afford it. This is a classic relationship attitude. In a partnership he shares his desire because his wife will be impacted emotionally and psychologically by his prospective purchase. Maybe she feels that it is too showy. Maybe she feels that it is wasteful. Maybe she doesn't like this brand of car. Maybe she wants to go away with him on a trip to Greece and she feels they are missing an intimacy that she yearns for. Maybe she feels that buying the car is driving a deeper wedge between them as he goes deeper into the world of things and she goes more deeply into the world of spirit or art or humanism or whatever. Her reactions to the possibility of the new car are important to him whether he likes them or not. Ignoring her is not partnership. This does not mean that he automatically does not buy the car. It means that the purchase comes out of their joint exploration of what the car means to each of them.

By now you might well be saying: "My God, who has time to talk over everything? I'm too busy! Besides, it is *my* money. I earned it and I can afford it. I don't want to be beholden to anyone." This is a fairly typical answer given by people who are in this situation. From our observations, it appears that everyone is too busy too much of the time. Maybe it is time to become less busy and spend more time deepening partnership and using partnership to discover more of who we are. It is true that Carlos can do what he wants with his money. If he wants a real partnership, however, Maria's feelings must be considered.

What are some of the basic areas that need to be considered in regard to finances?

Agreement to Share Financial Information

Once they are together, partners must each have a complete picture of the entire financial situation (both individual and joint) unless they have agreed beforehand to keep certain of their previous assets private and undisclosed. There is no right or wrong in this. It is only a question of making clear choices. Unconscious resentment and distrust are the alternatives.

Joint Approval of Major Financial Expenditures

When money is jointly held in a partnership, we recommend that all major expenditures be jointly approved. So long as a couple is still bouncing back and forth about whether or not to make a major expenditure, our experience is that it is best to wait until this "bouncing" has stopped. If this means that an expenditure cannot be made, then so be it. We have noticed that most of the decisions that are regretted later are the ones that get made when people were still bouncing between the pros and cons of a particular decision. This is also good advice for individuals who are in conflict about a decision.

Decision Making As an Opportunity for Discovery

Let's go back to Carlos and his money-spending ways. He now wants to buy a new boat and Maria is very much opposed. We now have a conflict that escalates into a nasty mess between them. Maria is furious because Carlos is always spending, spending, and spending. Carlos is furious because Maria is so controlling and is trying to regulate his life. If Carlos and Maria read this book and begin to apply what they learn, some interesting things may happen. What is the underlying vulnerability that they both have? Maria came from a poor family where spending was not possible. She is always afraid of not having anything, no matter how much Carlos has in the bank. Besides this, from her perspective it is his money and not hers. Her parents were always in debt and she still remembers the embarrassment and shame of having people chasing her father because of debts. Maria also has a different value system about money. She doesn't feel good about spending when there are so many people in the world who are impoverished.

As Maria and Carlos begin to approach their conflict in this way, they will learn to deal with the issues of underlying vulnerability and also to identify the disowned selves they carry for each other. Maria clearly feels that she is "not entitled" to the good things of life whereas Carlos definitely feels that he is entitled to have whatever he wants. They represent polar opposites in this matter and each needs some of what the other one carries. Suddenly an argument over finances and a new boat becomes a creative drama in which both parties can learn something about themselves. Carlos has disowned his vulnerability and he does not feel any concern about getting into debt or overextending himself financially. Carlos has no boundaries when it comes to money. He disowns the "no" in him that sees the possibility that a new boat is not necessary, is not important, and most definitely is a bad move financially. He needs Maria to teach him how to say no just as Maria needs him to teach her how to say yes.

Coming to some of these insights with each other will bring a new focus to the discussion and the partners' final choice will come from a place of clarity and alignment rather than from a war between two opposing primary selves in which the strongest wins. As we have said over and over again in so many different contexts, the issue is not whether or not Carlos should buy the boat. The issue is what part of him wants to buy it and what self or selves in Maria say no. Understanding this issue is like stepping out of the dark impenetrable jungle into a land of bright clear sunlight in which the most tangled underbrush can be cleared away.

Paying the Bills

When it comes to finances, one partner is usually stronger and better organized than the other. This is not a problem so long as there is no abdication of authority. The real issue is the personality differences that exist between the two people involved. Carlos wants to give Maria money every month for household expenses and he wants her to pay all the bills and not bother him with any of this. If she needs more money she can ask him for more money. Because of her background, Maria wants a real budget so that she knows how much they are spending and how much they have. Carlos is caught in an older, more patriarchal psychology and this is especially true in the field of money. He has established a strongly parental marriage relationship. It is our experience that if you want to see the patriarchy in action in its full glory, just look at the way people handle their finances.

Couples need to work out the basics of how they are going to work together before they can work out how the bills are going to be paid and how budgeting is going to be handled, if at all. Maria can create a household budget with the money that Carlos gives her, but, at some level, she is going to resent his total control of the over-all financial situation. So long as she has to ask him for money whenever she needs it, she is a daughter to his father self. For Carlos to expect that she is going to be a "good daughter" during the day and then a marvelously sexual "woman" at night is unrealistic. Control and power issues are more strongly entrenched in the financial side of relationship than any other place other than sexuality. These power issues must be solved before proper agreements can be reached in regard to how the bills are going to be paid and budgets developed.

THE BUSINESS MODEL IN ACTION

The recognition that relationship requires a business as well as a personal approach is a requirement of the partnering model. This requires time and energy. We cannot move out of the default program that was built into our systems early in life without a commitment to take the time that is needed to study the situation and make the appropriate new choices.

This is not easy because most of us have become so busy in our everyday lives. We say, "I'm too busy to take time to have business meetings like the ones you talk about." So the relationship remains locked in a self-perpetuating default program and we continue to be driven by inner and outer expectations to do more and more. We fulfill role requirements that really have nothing to do with who we are or what we want out of our lives and our relationships. We fill our calendars until there is no more room and soon we reach a point where we cannot bear to look at an empty calendar space so we compulsively fill it in with a new activity.

There is much written today about finding your soul reality. We will give you a very easy formula for discovering your soul, a formula that is simple beyond belief. Separate from the pushers of the world, both inner and outer. Get off the psychological freeway that you have been driving full time and try some of the country roads. Discover how so much of your busyness is based on your own vulnerability, something that you know very little about. Once you are off the full-time freeway, you will be amazed how your sense of soul begins to emerge and a feeling of fullness and holiness begins to be yours, both alone and in your relationship.

We have gone through our own phases of being too busy and we have paid the price in ourselves and in our relationship many different times. This we can say to you: *If you want a relationship that is intimate and fulfilling, where being together feeds you like a full and delicious meal, where a soul reality is a part of your ongoing interactions, then you must work together to create the space and time your relationship needs.* These business meetings give you a way to deal with the overwhelming details of modern life as true partners. Business leaders have meetings constantly to run their businesses properly and to achieve their goals. Is your partnership any less important? We think not.

Chapter 8

PARTNERING AND PARENTING: A COUPLE'S GUIDE TO ROMANCE

It is very easy for couples to lose their relationship when they have children. They become parents rather than partners. We believe that the connection between parents and their children is extremely important. But the connection between the partners is even more important. Their relationship must remain vital for the family system to be healthy, nourishing, and solid. If the primary linkage between the partners is lost, the entire family will suffer.

The arrival of a new baby is truly a blessed event. For many women, the birth of their first child opens them to unexpected new depths of love and devotion. Never before have they felt so unconditionally loved and accepted by another human being. And never before have they felt so unique and irreplaceable, so needed. Now that fathers have also been admitted to the mysteries of childbirth and are fully participating in fatherhood, they, too, often share in these feelings.

These feelings are intense and archetypal. They are holy and

they are practical. You can experience the sense of holiness sur-
rounding the mother-child connection in the sacred art of our culture, in the many magnificent paintings, sculptures, and stained
glass representations of the Madonna and child. But there is also a
bottom-line species-preserving practicality about this mother-child
connection. If a mother does not bond properly to her infant, the
child will not flourish. We need our mothers to bond to their children so that there will *be* a next generation.

With all of this pull toward the mother-child connection, you
can just imagine what happens to the man-woman partnering with
the arrival of children. The intensity of the linkage between the
partners is frequently lost as one, or both, of them shifts their primary linkage from the partner to the child or children. As a matter
of fact, many couples say that their marriage ended with the birth
of their first child.

You can see how the addition of children to a relationship poses
a major challenge. We believe that the connection between parents
and their children is extremely important. But the connection
between the partners is even more important. Their relationship must
remain vital for the family system to be strong, supportive, and nourishing. If the primary linkage between the partners is lost, the entire
family will suffer. This is true whether both partners are the natural
parents or one is a stepparent. Maintaining the primary linkage
between partners while, at the same time, giving the parent-child
connection the attention it requires is difficult but not impossible.

THE NEW CHILD

When the first child is born, the primary linkage that has existed
between the partners is disrupted and the new mother's primary
linkage automatically shifts to the baby. This is perfectly natural and
absolutely necessary — at least for a time. The new mother must
bond with the new baby in order for it to flourish. However, in order
for the relationship to survive intact, the energetic linkage to her
partner must not be permitted to deteriorate. We will use a typical

family situation to illustrate how this works.

Elyse and Edward were married for five years before Emily was born. They had had a passionate courtship and were intensely devoted to one another. Both were well-established professionals who had waited for marriage and children until an "appropriate" time. Elyse, age thirty-seven, was a successful lawyer and Edward, age forty-four, was an accomplished architect. They lived a comfortable upscale life in New York City. When Emily was born, Elyse made arrangements for an excellent nanny to help her. She and Edward expected their relationship to continue as it was in the past, sensible, intensely devoted, and sexual. They were very well organized adults who could deal effectively and efficiently with disruptions.

But Elyse and Edward had a surprise in store for them. They did not realize what would happen with the birth of Emily. Both were totally enchanted with this amazing new being. They had been rational people, and suddenly here they were, as foolishly emotional as the other new parents they had mocked previously. The result of this was a loss of the energetic linkage that had existed between them. Since they did not know about linkage, they did not know this was happening.

So it was that the primary linkage shifted from their relationship with each other to Emily. Now each partner was intensely linked with the new baby. Elyse and Edward were still fond of one another and they did not notice the change in their relationship. But it had most definitely changed. Everything still looked good from the outside. They were a happy and devoted family. But there was a problem, a problem so often faced when the first child is born. The energetic linkage changes and it is as though the marriage is no longer between the parents but is now between parent and child.

Traditionally, this shift in linkage is most noticeable in the woman. When the first child is born, she naturally links to the child, shifting her energies away from her husband. Her husband feels abandoned but, since he does not know much about his feelings, he does not know that he feels abandoned. But he must be nourished. He must link in somewhere to get fed. If he is denied energetic linkage with his wife, he links in elsewhere. This is often the time that the husband has his first affair.

However, the linkage is not always sexual. The husband can link to someone at work on an emotional, not a physical, level. He might link to the group at work, to his clients, to the work itself, to his computer, to his TV set, to the Internet, to the stock market, to another person, etc. He will establish a connection to whatever it is that makes him feel good. As he connects elsewhere, his wife feels abandoned. She connects more deeply to the new child. The husband feels more abandoned, and connects more intensely outside of the marriage. It is indeed a vicious cycle.

WHERE DOES THE LINKAGE GO?

Quite frequently, the linkage stays within the family and just moves to a different family member. It is not uncommon for the father to bond to a daughter and the mother to a son. Sometimes the father links to the firstborn and the mother to the youngest child. The father may establish linkage with the strongest or most competent child while the mother links to the one who needs her most. Either partner is most likely to form the strongest linkage with the child who carries his or her disowned selves.

Whether we are dealing with blended families, adoptive families, or families of origin, there is often a tremendous amount of feeling about these primary linkages. Who is the father's favorite? Who is the mother's favorite? What about the siblings? There are many painful conflicting loyalties that pull family members in a variety of directions.

When the Father's Primary Linkage Goes to the Daughter

The most frequent reaction of a husband who feels abandoned (but does not know it) is to switch his primary linkage from his wife to his daughter. This is what happened with Don. We will tell you his story because it is so common. It is a story we have heard repeated over and over again by grown women and men. It is a story that carries pain for everyone involved. If you, or one of your children or one of your siblings, were in a relationship of this type, it helps to know what was going on.

Don was a rather shy stock analyst who was more comfortable with his charts than with people. He had married Eva when he was twenty-five years old and she was twenty-seven. In his eyes, Eva was a woman of the world, sexual, outgoing, lovingly caring, and confident. He adored her and they had a very good marriage. He felt wonderfully nourished and safe with Eva.

With the birth of their son, Evan, Eva's attention shifted. Their sex life dwindled as Eva's primary linkage went to the new baby. Don felt a bit left out, but he could not bring himself to say anything to Eva even though he yearned for their old closeness. Don began to spend more time at work but, since he was basically a loner, he never made any strong connections there. With the birth of their second child, a daughter named Aurora, Don found somebody new to love. His energetic linkage shifted from his wife to the new child. He adored Aurora just as he had previously adored her mother.

Don and Aurora were inseparable. They did everything together. She was his special "little girl" and he was her beloved "Daddy." She could make him smile when nobody else could and she, in turn, always felt safe and happy when he was around. Aurora took care of Don's needs (proudly bringing him his coffee in the morning) and he took care of hers (patiently helping her with her homework at night). Although there was nothing improper or sexual about their connection, it was very deep. They were — in an energetic sense — married to one another. Eva, in turn, remained linked energetically to Evan.

But life moves on and nothing stays the same. Aurora's hormones began to percolate, as they do around the age of thirteen, and she found herself longing to spend more time with her friends and less with her father. By the age of fourteen, Aurora's sexuality was beginning to blossom and she was looking like a little woman. She was also beginning to notice boys who, in turn, noticed her. The innocent paradise of the father-daughter connection was about to be disrupted.

Don was, as we have said, a shy, nonpsychological man, and he did not realize what was happening. He saw that his daughter was turning into a woman and this was unsettling to him. He was totally unprepared for some of the feelings that began to bubble up in him. He was horrified to notice that there were times when he found Aurora attractive and even experienced sexual feelings when she would hug him or sit in his lap. He was a very principled man and he did not know what to do. No one had ever spoken about this as a natural event or taught him how to behave. He was deeply ashamed.

Not only was Aurora turning into a woman before his very eyes, she was also withdrawing her energy from him just as Eva had so many years before. She was more interested in her friends than in her family. She was not always at home and available when he wanted her companionship. She no longer took care of him in the old way. As a matter of fact, she stopped her morning ritual of bringing him his coffee. Don did not know about his own vulnerability, he did not know about his feelings of abandonment. If he did, he might have reacted differently and maintained his energetic connection with his daughter while he dealt with this change in the form of their relationship and the challenge of her transition into womanhood.

Instead, as so many fathers have done in the past and more will do in the future, Don broke his energetic linkage with Aurora. He withdrew his affection and became cool. He became critical of her — of her looks, her feelings, and her behavior. Sometimes he criticized her out loud and sometimes she would just see it in his eyes or feel it in his manner. He was particularly critical of her friends and her budding sexuality. He made her feel ashamed and wrong.

Don was no longer available to spend time with Aurora even when she needed him. He lost interest in her schoolwork and her other accomplishments. He told her that she was too old for him to hug any more. Suddenly, at the age of fourteen, Aurora lost her father and she did not know what she had done. All she knew — very vaguely — was that it must have had something to do with the fact that she was no longer a little girl, that she had become a woman, and that there must be something wrong with being a woman.

This is a deep loss for the fathers and the daughters of the world. However, if the primary linkage had remained where it belonged, between Don and his wife, Eva, this never would have happened. Don would never have "married" Aurora and Eva would never have "married" Evan. The children would never have become so special to their parents and neither child would have had the responsibility for the well-being of the parent. Eva and Don would have remained partners to one another and the family system would have been able to work creatively with Aurora's move into womanhood (and Evan's move into manhood).

WHAT HAPPENS WHEN WE BECOME PARENTS RATHER THAN PARTNERS?

It is so easy for couples to lose their relationship when they have children, to become parents rather than partners! This usually happens without anyone noticing. Because this is so often the case, we want to give you an idea of what this looks like so that you can be alert to this often subtle shift in connection. Of course, there is one foolproof sign. If a couple calls one another "Mom" and "Pop" rather than by their given names, it is pretty clear that they have lost their partnership status. But there are more subtle signs.

Years ago, when we driving around in England, we spent the night in a magical coastal town where we attended a "medieval banquet." Just as in the Middle Ages, we were seated at long tables set with heaping platters of food that we shared with the other guests. The whole event was delightfully convivial, so we chatted with the young English couple seated opposite us. They were quite lovely and very young, but there was something missing. The connection between them was pleasant and respectful, but not as exciting or sensual as one might expect at their age. We wondered what was amiss and, as we talked with them, we soon discovered what had happened. They told us, with great pride in their excellent parenting, that this was their first night out together since the birth of their son, six years earlier. The mystery was solved! They had become parents rather than partners and they had lost their vital primary linkage with one another. The primary linkage of each partner had apparently shifted to the son.

What are some of the signs that this has happened in a relationship?

• You have lost the sense of the magic of your own relationship. Your child — and your relationship to this child — has all the magic.

• Being alone with your partner is no longer a priority.

• Your children are entitled to everything. You and your partner must put yourselves, your needs, and your relationship in second place.

• You never go anywhere without the children. You can hardly remember the last time you went to a restaurant or a movie alone.

• You cannot imagine a vacation without your children.

• You cannot even think of spending an overnight by yourselves.

• If you do go out without the children, you talk about them, or think about them, during the time that you are away. It is as though you never left them.

• There is no privacy in the house, no space where you can be together without the possibility of interruption.

• There is no special space or time for you to be sexually

or sensually intimate.

• The children have complete access to you all the time. Nothing is off limits to them.

• You find yourself more aligned with your child than with your partner. In a conflict, you always see your child's point of view rather than your partner's.

• You feel that your child understands you better than your partner does.

• You feel a deeper connection with your child than with your partner.

This change in linkage can come with the birth of the child or it can develop gradually over time. Whichever way it starts, it is an ever-accelerating process. *The more you and your partner drift apart, the more each of you will link with one or more of the children. The more you link with the child, the more you will drift apart from your partner. The cycle never ends.* The result is that each of you — your partner and yourself — ends up in a primary relationship with one of the children. It is as though you are married to the child rather than to one another.

WHAT CAN YOU DO TO KEEP YOUR RELATIONSHIP PRIMARY?

First of all, it is okay to keep the children. It is okay to keep your partner as well. This is one of those times when you can have your cake and eat it too. It is not always easy, it often involves doing something different or unfamiliar, or even taking the chance of hurting somebody's feelings, but it is definitely worth the discomfort. Keeping your relationship primary always takes planning. Sometimes the plans get pretty complex but, again, it is worth the effort.

We have found that there are a few very practical steps you can take to keep your partnership alive and your energetic linkage primary. Here are some to think about. We suggest that you follow these and then add some of your own ideas.

• *Remember always that your basic commitment is to support, maintain, and deepen your relationship as partners even though you have children.* Be aware that your relationship and the ultimate well-being of your family depend upon the maintenance of your energetic linkage as partners. A solid relationship between parents is the best medicine for any family system.

• *Be alert to the loss of energetic linkage with your partner.* What usually happens is that one *(not both)* of the partners feels the loss of linkage in the relationship. If you feel this slippage, do not ignore it and do not deny it. Do something about it. Be selfish. Do not become understanding. Do not feel embarrassed or think that you are not entitled to want more from your partner. Do not allow yourself to excuse your partner by thinking something like, "She (he) is so busy, I don't want to burden her (him) with even more demands." If your partner is the one to sense the loss of linkage and speaks to you about it, do not feel guilty and do not be defensive. There's really nothing wrong. You haven't been a "naughty child." This is a natural part of life. It only means that your partner misses you. It is actually a compliment that your partner is sensitive to the quality of your relationship and cares enough to want the linkage restored. Try to plan together how you might do this.

• *Create regularly scheduled special rituals.* These do not have to be earthshaking or profound, but they should give you the experience of being together as though you were on a date. They do not have to intrude upon the rest of the family. We, for instance, had a regular date for an early breakfast every Tuesday morning for years. It was fun and it was special. It came first. We never scheduled anything else early on a Tuesday morning. The children all knew about our Tuesday morning breakfasts at Sportsman's Lodge and it was a part of the family tradition. Try to think of something that might work for you.

• *Take time to be alone together, preferably away from the home.* The home is the place of the family and it is all too easy to turn into parents when you are at home and to lose the feeling of being lovers. It is amazing how restorative an overnight away from home can be. Or, if you can't manage an overnight, how about an afternoon assignation with your spouse? You could go to a hotel for a couple of hours in the afternoon and then return to work. Mightn't that feel deliciously naughty? You don't have to go far. We suggest that you do something along these lines at least once a month. If there is no way that you can leave the house, then have the children go elsewhere for an overnight. These can be special times for them as well as for you. They can visit with family or friends. You can trade overnights with other parents who could also use some time alone. Be creative.

• *Protect your intimate times together; do not allow your responsibilities as a parent to drive out your enjoyment of sensuality and sexuality.* It is good to remember that you and your partner are lovers. Create the ability to have privacy in your home. We strongly suggest a lock on the bedroom door. You do not have to use it all the time, but it certainly helps when you do not want to be interrupted unexpectedly. This is particularly nice when you want to be physically intimate. You can relax and enjoy yourselves more completely when you know that there is no chance of looking up at a critical moment and finding a little face (or faces) looking down at you.

• *Claim "time alone" as parents and make this a part of family life.* There are other times when you need to be alone together that are not sexual. Relationships take time. Energetic linkage takes time. Being quiet together takes time. The practicalities of running a household take time. For all of these, you need time to be together without interruption. Protect this time. Teach your children that there are times you need to be alone. You do not have to be cruel or dismissive about this, just let your children know when you need some "time alone." They can learn to respect this and then, in turn, when they are parents they will know how to take this kind of time with their own partners.

• *In short, remember to honor your relationship and keep it healthy.*

BUT HOW CAN I TELL THIS TO MY CHILDREN?

You may be thinking to yourself, "These are pretty good ideas, but what in the world am I to tell my children?" It's amazing how terrifying this prospect can be! Whatever will you tell them? How do you let your children know that you need time alone? How do you get them to understand why this is necessary for us as adults and how, in turn, it will benefit them? What exactly do you tell them you will be *doing* when you're away overnight? How do you explain the need for romance to a six-year-old? Worse yet, to your thirteen-year-old who is struggling with a case of galloping puberty? How do you get your three-year-old to understand that you need time to reconnect with somebody other than her?

If these questions make your blood run cold, then you are like most parents. You do not feel entitled to have a life of your own, one that is independent of your children. Their needs come first and yours lag behind. We would suggest that, before you think about communicating these ideas to your children, you realize how much feeling all this stirs up in you. Know that you are entitled to the kind of relationship we're talking about in this chapter. We're happy to say that this is as good for your children as it is for you.

Now relax and take a deep breath. Make this project of communicating to your children a part of your partnering. If you do this as a team, you will feel much better about it and you will be more effective. Have a meeting and decide together how you will do this and what you will say. Think things through. As with any setting of boundaries, weigh the consequences of your own actions. Pay attention to both sides of yourselves — the sides of you that are totally involved with the children and want to be sure this is done well, and the sides of you that are primarily interested in the relationship and might not pay much attention to the children's needs. Remember that this balance is important. You are keeping the needs and feelings of your children in mind while you are claiming time and space for your adult partnering relationship.

Our idea is to approach this in much the same way as when you explained to your children why you go to work. That will put you in a more objective frame of mind and many of your discomforts will dissolve. You are dealing with some very similar issues. Basically you are telling your children that they are not in charge of your lives, you are setting boundaries and, at the same time, you are letting them know that they are also very important to you. The underlying principle is that what is good for the relationship is good for the family system. Think of it as you would a good job; it contributes to everyone's well-being.

How did you explain to your children about having to go to work and leaving them behind? We're willing to bet that you didn't suffer much guilt over this. You were probably very matter-of-fact. You just explained that grown-ups go to work. They go to work in the morning and come back at night. Since you know that this separation can be difficult for children, and we might add, a bit difficult for you when they're being particularly delicious, you might have even developed some rituals that help with this transition.

Our grandchildren have a very sweet ritual for the times when their parents leave the house. The children (accompanied by who-ever is staying with them) go to the window, climb up on the couch beneath it, wave to their parents, and shout good-bye. Their parents look up and wave back. Then the children climb down from the couch, run to the next window, and wave and shout good-bye again while the parents wave back. The children feel very grown-up and very much a part of things, and the leave-taking is easier for the parents as well.

Inevitably, your children will ask what you are going to do when you are not with them. Watch out for the need to explain your actions and to justify them. Again, let's think about work. When parents go to work, they do things. They often cannot tell their children what they do or how they do it. It's just too complex to explain what you do as a lawyer, or a psychologist, or an econ-omist. They are not going to understand. You explain your absence in some age-appropriate fashion. You tell the two-year-old that you are going away tonight and that Grandma or their baby-sitter, Cathy, is going to be there with them. Explain this in the same kind of matter-of-fact way that you would explain a business trip.

With older children you might want to speak with them about the need for parents to have time alone with one another. This will help to teach them good partnering skills for their adult relation-ships. Explain the idea of time alone in two ways. First, let them know the practical nature of your time together; it gives you time to arrange for the business details of everyday living. For instance, you need time to talk about the new house that all of you are going to enjoy. Second, let them know the importance of the feeling part of your relationship, that your relationship is the foundation of the home. You can explain that this time alone helps you to feel good with each other or closer to each other or even to work out dis-agreements in private. Let them know that this is important because when you are happy with each other you can build a healthy, solid home in which everything works better.

Of course, it helps if this idea of time alone for parents is set up early in life. If it has been a part of the family expectations from the very beginning, children accept it easily and they actually *know* how good it is for everyone. You might never have to explain anything. Children are pretty observant and they notice that parents are usually more cheerful and relaxed after their time alone. But, whenever you do it, claiming time for yourselves and your relationship is not much different from setting any other kind of boundary. Do it as a team with forethought and conviction, in a matter-of-fact fashion, and, last but not least, with energetic linkage to your children.

Your ability to honor your relationship and to claim time for yourselves gives your children a good example to follow. You will find that they learn early to set their own boundaries easily and gracefully and to take time for their own important relationships. It can actually be quite charming. For instance, two-year-old Haley, in much the same voice that her parents use toward her, explained sweetly to us, "I'll be with you in a few minutes. I'm busy talking to Elmo (her favorite doll) right now about the new house." She quickly finished her conversation with Elmo and then she was ready for us.

As we have said, making your relationship a priority is extremely important. You do not have to apologize for this, since a good partnering relationship provides the foundation for a healthy family home. In order for you to maintain a vital and intimate partnering relationship, you must create proper boundaries that separate your adult relationship from the relationship you have with your children. This is very reassuring to everyone. Roles are clearly defined and boundaries are intact and appropriate. The home feels solid.

Everything we have discussed in this chapter is as true for stepfamilies and adoptive families as it is for families of origin. Now that you have seen the impact that children can have on relationships and we have given you some ideas about combining child rearing with relationship, let's move on to consider some other major challenges that our relationships face in the world today.

Chapter 9

THE TOP TEN CHALLENGES TO RELATIONSHIP: KEEPING YOUR LOVE ALIVE AMID LIFE'S ROUTINES

The basic requirement for the care and feeding of a relationship is this: Partners must make the linkage — or connection — between them a priority in their lives.

There are many challenges to relationship; some of them come from outside of us and some come from within. We are going to show you the top ten challenges so that you can recognize them and do something about them. Meeting these challenges takes commitment, time, and effort. But a good relationship is well worth this effort and, we might point out, a great deal of this effort can be fun.

There is one very simple principle to keep in mind. The basic requirement for the care and feeding of a relationship is this: Partners must make the linkage — or connection — between them a priority in their lives. If they do so, the relationship will flourish. Anything that disrupts this linkage will disrupt their relationship.

Even the most devoted of partners will have interests other than their relationship and they will form attachments and linkages elsewhere. This is an important part of life. However, if your primary linkage in life shifts away from your partner and remains elsewhere, it is likely to prove fatal to your relationship.

There is a great deal of competition for our attention. All of us have a great many distractions in our lives and we do not have to go far to find something that will divert our attention from our partners. We will describe the ten major distractions that we have seen over the years. At the end of each of these, we will give you a chance to answer the question: Where is your primary linkage? You can use these questions to look at your own relationship to determine which among these are your major challenges.

Each of us has a different style. If you are the kind of person who likes to take time to think about these issues, read this chapter at a time when you can be quiet and alone. Give yourself time to think about the questions and write your answers in your notebook. If, however, you like to do things quickly, just read this with a highlight pen in hand. See what comes to mind as you read. Highlight whatever speaks to you and make notes in the margin of the book — or on Post-It notes if you need more space.

Now, on to the challenges.

CHALLENGE 1: TELEVISION

Most homes have a television set. Actually, many homes have more than one so that each family member has a set all to himself or herself. This is a very compelling distraction. Television sets and television programs are designed to attract us and keep our attention. That is their goal. The entire industry is based upon linking us irrevocably to the TV set. They seduce us with the weekly shows, the news, the stock market, our favorite ball team, the Olympics, the latest scandal, our favorite soap opera, that special program we cannot miss. Others among us are seduced by the sheer power inherent in the remote control. We are in charge! We can do or watch whatever we like, whenever we like. We can change channels to our hearts content without anybody scolding us. We are not forced to finish anything.

In addition to this seductive quality of television, there is its lack of confrontation and complication. It essentially complements your every mood and gives you whatever you want, whenever you want it. After all, has your TV ever made demands on you? Has it ever been disappointed in you? Has it ever criticized you? Has it made you feel vulnerable? Does it pressure you to finish anything? Does it frighten you or make you feel insecure? Do its feelings get hurt? Does it ever disagree with you? In short, there is no way that a TV set makes you as uncomfortable as your partner can!

Is it any wonder that we frequently find partners spending a great deal more time linked energetically to the TV than to one another?

Think about it! Are you more attached to your TV than to your partner? Which would you rather do without?

If you would rather do without your partner, it seems safe to say that something is missing in your relationship. We find that one of the first things to disappear in a relationship is time together. Both partners get so busy that they forget each other. Life today is difficult and demanding. People are usually so overworked, over-stressed, or exhausted that when they do have a moment, they drop into a comfortable chair and watch TV. It takes real effort to stay on your feet and do something different.

The TV is very seductive and the relaxation and entertainment it provides can be essential and restorative, but linkage is linkage and our relationships need adequate energetic linkage in order to be healthy and thrive. You might even try for linkage while you're watching TV together. How about making physical contact with one another as you watch? Perhaps you could curl up together in a big comfortable chair or on a couch.

The most important challenge is to find time to really be together in energetic linkage, however you do it. Be creative. How about making plans for doing something together away from the TV? For instance, going to a movie is a different experience from watching the same movie on TV. It's a date, it's going out together, and it means getting out of the house. There is always some way to be together even if you have a limited amount of time and money. Take a walk, go to a park, run errands together, go to the supermarket at an odd hour when it's empty and you're not too rushed, take three minutes to watch the sunset. And whenever possible, take some time to sit together just to be quiet, or to talk over the day's happenings.

CHALLENGE 2: WORK

Our work is very important. It gives us power and money and keeps us safe in the world. It gives us the satisfaction of feeling that we are making a contribution, and may even give our lives a sense of meaning and purpose. It helps us to define ourselves. Hopefully, if we give it enough attention, our work will always be there to support us and we do not have to worry about our work abandoning or divorcing us. Most important, as long as we have our work, we do not have to think very much about our vulnerability. Anything that helps us to deal with our vulnerability, without us having to face it directly, is extremely attractive.

Is it any wonder that many of us develop a primary linkage to our work and relegate our relationship to second place? When we feel vulnerable deep down inside and we do not want to know about it, going to work can make us feel better. At work, we make a difference. We are needed. We are wanted. Here we have mastery, or at least we can work toward mastery. This is extremely reassuring. Life feels safe and structured and our priorities are set for us. We know what is expected and we are able to do the right thing. Add to all this the fact that we are earning money and contributing to the financial security of both our inner and outer children, and you have a total win-win situation.

Unfortunately, the more our linkage is to work, the less energy there is left for relationship. Since the lifeblood of any relationship is linkage, this is not good for the relationship! The tendency to link to work rather than to one's partner is a major challenge to relationship.

Traditionally, men have buried themselves in work when they felt vulnerable or their emotions became too uncomfortable. Now women, too, have this marvelous option available. Many women have learned to drop the linkage in the relationship and shift their energies to their work. When the going gets rough for a two-career couple and each partner has satisfying work, there is a strong temptation for the partners to shift the primary linkage from their relationship to their work. As this happens, each feels abandoned by the other and each links even more intensely to work.

This linkage may be to the work itself, to the clients they serve, or to their coworkers. This linkage is frequently to a particular person at work, an understanding coworker or a particularly supportive assistant. Traditionally it was the man's secretary. This may or may not become a full-blown extramarital relationship.

We find this can be a particularly subtle challenge for people who work together. For instance, it is very easy for the two of us to get so involved in a project that we lose contact with each other. We may both get so interested in our writing that our linkage goes to the book rather than to one another. It may look as though we are still in a relationship because we are both linked to the same object, but we are not. Not really. We are like two oxen yoked to the same cart. We are pulling together and doing a great job, but we have blinders on and we no longer see each other. We just see the road ahead. When this happens, there is a loss of intimacy. We do not feel good and we do not know why.

There are many times in life when being linked to work looks like a natural and necessary move. This is particularly true when there are financial pressures, either real or imagined. One or both partners will deal with this underlying vulnerability in the most seemingly sensible fashion by working harder and earning more money. This is not a problem if the connection between the partners stays strong and intimate. Usually, however, at times like these the truly strong connection switches to work and the partners gradually and unobtrusively drift apart until they are almost like strangers to one another.

Of course, there are times when any of us will feel better at work than at home, but think about it: Overall, where do *you* feel better, with your partner or with your work?

To deal with this challenge, see what you can do about putting a limit on the amount of time you spend at work or thinking about work. Set boundaries. Try to set realistic time limits that you can meet; for instance, no work or work-related activity between 8:30 P.M. and 7:00 A.M. This will probably be extremely difficult to do at first. To help you do this, keep a notepad with you so that when you have a work-related thought during your off-hours, you can write it down and not think about it until the next work session. For instance, you remember that you should send an E-mail to double-check on yesterday's order. Write it down on your notepad and put it away until tomorrow. Otherwise you will probably spend a great deal of time (1) trying not to think this thought and (2) fearing that you will forget to send the E-mail.

CHALLENGE 3:
OTHER RELATIONSHIPS IN FACT AND FANTASY

There was a period in the late 1960s and early 1970s when people realized that they could not expect a single romantic or sexual relationship to meet all their needs. This was a reaction against earlier overidealized expectations of marriages "made in heaven" and dreams of "happily ever after" when all that was needed was one Cinderella and one Prince Charming. It was a time of cultural revolution during which there was a good deal of experimentation with extramarital relationships and deep extramarital friendships.

Quite often this worked beautifully for a while. Each partner felt more alive and fulfilled. They brought back new energy to the primary relationship and the linkage between the partners intensified.

But what we noticed during those years was that, sooner or later, the linkage between the partners began to dissipate as the linkage to outsiders increased in intensity. Most of the time the primary linkage finally shifted from the partner to someone else.

As normal, ordinary human beings, we can expect to feel attractions to people other than our partners. This is totally natural. It just means that we are alive and that our hormones are functioning properly. There is a great deal to be learned from these attractions if we do not panic about them or feel too guilty.

There was definitely a kernel of truth in the thinking of the sixties and seventies. One person does not hold everything; therefore one relationship cannot hold everything. We have our primary selves and we have our disowned selves. In our relationships there are selves that are acceptable or primary and others that both partners disown.

If you think about what we said earlier regarding disowned selves (see chapter 2), you get the picture of what happens in relationship. Our disowned selves, and the disowned selves of our partners, are the selves that we find fascinating in others. These are the selves that exert the fatal attractions that cause us to drop the linkage to our partners and develop a primary linkage elsewhere. *This linkage does not have to become sexual in order to challenge the relationship. It just needs to be primary.*

Sometimes this is not even a linkage to an actual person, sexual or otherwise. Sometimes it is a preoccupation with a fantasy. One of the partners develops a strong fantasy life and disappears into it. This can be a fantasy about another person, about an imagined person, or a fantasy about a different kind of life. *The primary linkage shifts from the relationship or the partnering to this fantasy or this fantasy character.* For some people, this can be as strong an involvement as an involvement with another person and it can disrupt the linkage between partners as much as an actual affair. Just as in an actual affair, the primary linkage has been shifted. Here, the primary linkage is to the fantasy rather than to the partner. Where does this linkage go? Just as in an affair or an attraction, the linkage is always to a person or a situation that is carrying a disowned self.

What can be done to reestablish the linkage within the partnership? If you follow our thinking, look for the disowned selves that are operating. What is it that is irresistible about this person who is not your partner? Where does this person carry either your disowned self or that of your partner? You can actually use this attraction as a teacher, and either you or your partner can claim the disowned self so that this irresistible attraction becomes more resistible and your primary linkage returns to the relationship. What does this look like? Perhaps you and your partner have become rather complacent and predictable. Your routine is safe and comfortable because each of you has disowned your spontaneity and wildness. We might expect that someone who is more spontaneous or unpredictable would be very attractive to one or both of you. If you take this attraction as a sign that you need a bit of fresh air and that your lives need a bit of change, you may be able to incorporate this change *into* your relationship rather than changing relationships.

These missing pieces that we find irresistible in others can be almost anything. Each of us is different. The person who carries this attraction can be a rebel or a conservative, sexual or proper, a professional or a homebody, fiscally responsible or fiscally impulsive, cautious or spontaneous, thoughtful or selfish, powerful or sensitive, passionate or cool, sophisticated or simple. The list goes on forever, but we just wanted to give you a picture of the variety of possibilities.

Think of the people in your life who exert a fascination over you and who pull your energetic linkage toward themselves and away from your partner. What is it that they carry that is missing in you, your partner, or the relationship? How might you bring more balance into your life and into your relationship by including some of this missing energy?

CHALLENGE 4: FRIENDS

It is extremely important to have friends and not to depend solely upon your partner to fill all your interpersonal needs. However, it is possible for our friendships to divert our primary linkage to someone other than our partner.

In the past, this has been particularly true of women. Their friendships have been deeper and more intimate than their marriages. They felt that they could say anything to their friends, but that they had to be cautious about what they said to their husbands. When they needed comfort they spoke with their friends not with their husbands. When they were unhappy about something that their husbands said or did, they did not speak to their husbands about it, but aired their concerns with their friends instead. Rather than saying to their partners, "I did not like it when you…" they called their friends and discussed the matter with them. This shifts the primary linkage from the husband to the friend.

There is another way in which the primary linkage moves away from the relationship and to the friendship. This is a particular problem when one partner is an overly responsible person who gets very involved with the needs and problems of friends. There is a point where the balance between the friend and partner is shifted and the relationship loses. The energy is withdrawn from the partner and goes to the needy friend.

For instance, Bob and Jill are sitting at the dinner table. Jill tells Bob a funny story about their daughter's success with her potty training. Bob proudly tells Jill about his contract to build three homes in the new housing development in the next town. They are having a great time together. The phone rings. It is Jill's friend Marla, who is having marital problems — again. Rather than finishing her meal with Bob, Jill leaves him at the table and talks for an hour with Marla. She links to Marla, her friend who needs her. She breaks her linkage with Bob, who, she thinks, can manage on his own. If this happens frequently enough, the primary linkage is no longer in the marriage but in the friendship, and the marriage becomes an empty form rather than a living relationship.

As you might notice from this interchange, friends often carry our disowned selves, or missing pieces. If we look at the example of Bob and Jill, we see that Jill is not allowed to be needy like Marla. Jill, as a responsible type of person, must abandon her own dinner in order to care for Marla. She does not have the option of saying, "I'm sorry, but I can't talk just now. Bob and I are eating dinner. I'll call you back tomorrow."

The question to ask yourself here is, Who is my best friend? In general, when you have something really important on your mind would you rather talk to your partner or your friends? For a truly intimate relationship, the answer will be "my partner." There is a saying: "It's wonderful to be married to your best friend." When the primary linkage is in the relationship, that is just the way we feel; our partners are our best friends.

CHALLENGE 5: CHILDREN

We devoted chapter 8 to the effect of children on relationships because it is so common for children to replace the partner as our primary linkage. They are a marvelous gift but, just because they are so fascinating and delicious, they are also an almost irresistible distraction from the primary relationship. For many of us, it is the easiest thing in the world to shift our primary linkage from our partners to our children.

Basically, when a baby is born, the mother must bond to the new infant so that it will flourish. This usually means that, at least for a while, she will shift her primary linkage from the relationship to the child. These days with the increasing involvement of fathers in child rearing, the father is likely to shift his primary linkage to the child as well, for the same reason the mothers have done so in the past. It feels good.

It is absolutely necessary for both parents to realize how important it is for themselves, their relationship, and the well-being of their children, to stay connected to one another. This means that they will do whatever is necessary to maintain their own linkage.

When the linkage between partners is broken because one partner shifts the primary linkage to the child, the other partner is left hanging out alone, like an atom with an unpaired electron, commonly known as a free radical. This "free radical" will look for someone or something else to bond to. Then any of these other "challenges" we have been discussing may become the object of the primary linkage. Let's see what this can look like.

John and Jane have just had a baby after eight years of marriage. Before the birth of the child, John and Jane were inseparable. Jane taught school full time and John worked in computer software development. Now that the baby, Nancy, has entered the scene, Jane has taken a leave of absence from teaching, she is busy all the time and her primary linkage shifts from John to the baby. John feels rejected and is a bit worried about money, but he does not like to feel vulnerable so he does the sensible thing. He spends more and more time at work. After all, there are more bills to be paid and Jane is no longer teaching full time. Now Jane is linked to the baby and John is linked to his work. But there is a problem, a big one: their connection is no longer primary.

Sometimes the primary connection remains within the family but instead of being between the parents, it shifts to the children. Each partner links to a different child. The mother's primary connection may be to her son and the father's to his daughter. One parent may connect to the most successful child while the other parent's primary connection is to the most needy child. If there is a single child, it sometimes happens that both parents' primary linkage is to the same child.

We've observed that something similar to this can happen with pets. The primary connection remains in the household but it shifts from between the partners to the pet. There are even some people whose primary linkage has always been with their pets rather than with their partners. You can see them pouring all their loving, nurturing, personal energy into their pets — petting them, kissing them, talking to them in endearing tones — while the relationship with the partner is less physical, more cut off, more impersonal, and more businesslike. Again, it's not a question of whether or not to love your pets, it's just a question of who has your primary linkage.

If you have children, ask yourself these questions: Is your primary linkage to your partner or to your children? What about your partner's primary connection, is it to you or to a child? When did you and your partner last take time to be alone and to reconnect in intimate ways that did not include your children? (See chapter 8 for more suggestions about meeting this challenge.)

CHALLENGE 6: *DOING* RATHER THAN *BEING*

Most people have within them a pusher that pushes them to do more and more. They must learn more, accomplish more, earn more, be better, be smarter, expand, succeed, be the best. For our pushers, standing still is unacceptable. We must never waste a moment, we must always be doing something. When we reach one goal, our pusher sets another. There is no rest, just constant doing.

Unfortunately, this constant action makes linkage impossible. *You have to stop moving in order to connect to another human being.* This is not encouraged in our culture. We are not given permission to slow down long enough to connect with one another and to nourish our relationships. As a matter of fact, we are encouraged to move faster and faster. We're like the Red Queen from *Alice in Wonderland,* running as fast as we can to stay in the same place.

Now there is a new challenge to relationship. We have a New Age pusher, who, in addition to everything else, is pushing us toward growth, consciousness, greater spirituality, and, for the most ambitious of us, enlightenment. This New Age pusher will stop at nothing in its quest for growth. It has us learning about ourselves, working with our process, paying attention to our dreams, doing our spiritual practices, and following a myriad of new rules. It thinks nothing of breaking the connection to our partners and taking us away from them for months at a time.

Again, it is a matter of linkage. If the relationship connection remains primary, the partners will be able to handle the demands of this New Age pusher. However, if the primary linkage moves elsewhere, we are no longer linked to our partners and the relationship is severely challenged. When this happens, there is a chance that the relationship will not survive as our partners feel abandoned by the loss of connection and look for their linkage elsewhere.

CHALLENGE 7:
COMPUTERS — THE NEW MYSTICAL LOVER

There are many among us who cannot resist the glow of the computer screen or the lure of the Internet. There is so much to do, to see, and to learn. There is so much to explore. There is an endless opportunity for play. You plan to take a moment to check your E-mail or to reconcile your bank account, and five hours later you drag yourself to bed, exhausted but happy, hardly remembering your partner's name.

We have come to think of the computer as the new mystical lover, a seductive creature who, always awake and available, sings a siren song at all hours of the day and night.

Again, this is a question of linkage. No matter what you are working at, it's good-bye to your partner as your primary linkage shifts to the computer. Once when we were speaking about this as having an almost addictive quality, a computer expert told us he had heard that when people work on computers their brains move into a very satisfying alpha rhythm that is literally addictive. We do not know whether or not this is true, but it certainly seems that way.

There are many levels to this new fatal attraction. Some people have an intermittent linkage problem that does not constantly detract from their relationship. When they are working on their computers, that is their primary linkage but they are capable of returning and connecting to their partners. There are others, however, for whom the connection to the computer, and to the things that they access through their computer, is truly the primary linkage in their lives.

To check this out, ask yourself where you have more fun, with your computer or with your partner.

CHALLENGE 8: ALCOHOL AND DRUGS

Partners often use drugs or alcohol to relax with one another or to enhance and intensify their relationship, particularly its sexual aspects. This may work very well if these substances are used in moderation, but this, too, can present a challenge. There is a point during intoxication beyond which the intimate connection between the partners is lost and each one moves into his or her own private world. When this happens, the other partner is abandoned.

If drug or alcohol usage moves into the realm of an addiction, the relationship will suffer. In addition to whatever practical problems this presents in terms of overall functioning in the world, addictions break the connection between partners. *The addict's primary linkage is to the substance, not to the partner.*

Not only do we see a loss of connection between the partners, but there is an additional consequence of excessive drug or alcohol usage. The user loses boundaries (and judgment) and often links energetically with others in an inappropriate way, leaving the partner feeling even more alone and abandoned.

Pay attention to the quality of the connection between your partner and yourself when you have a few drinks. Do you tend to lose one another? You may need your partner to help you to figure this out. Our partners are often more sensitive to these changes than we are. Because of this, your partner may be able to tell you about a loss of connection that is not noticeable to you.

CHALLENGE 9:
BECOMING A PSYCHOLOGICAL KNOW-IT-ALL

Unfortunately, there can be a downside to this self-exploration and psychological work. It is entirely possible for us to lose our vulnerability as we gain knowledge and to eventually become a psychological know-it-all. As we accumulate information about our relationships, our partners, and ourselves, we move very naturally and smoothly into the role of the expert or advisor. And just as smoothly and naturally, we lose our linkage to our partners.

This means that we are no longer equals. We are no longer partners in a relationship where both people feel a bit vulnerable and both people are trying to find the answers. There is an expert and a novice. This is a foolproof way to break an intimate connection.

These experts simply cannot make a connection to others. That is not what they do. Instead, they instruct others. It does not matter one bit that their information may be brilliantly insightful and precisely on target. Accuracy is totally irrelevant! The energetic linkage is lost and so is the intimacy. The relationship withers from lack of connection. This is truly ironic because the harder that this psychological know-it-all works at fixing a relationship, the worse things get.

The best way to figure out whether this has happened to you is to look at the reactions of the people around you, particularly the reaction of your partner. Do people's eyes glaze over when you begin to share your insights with them? Do they become defensive, argumentative, or rebellious? If so, you have probably — unwittingly — become a psychological expert who approaches others with a great deal of information, but without any real connection.

CHALLENGE 10: MAINTAINING A PERFECT RELATIONSHIP

Sometimes we work too hard to keep everything in our relationships perfect. We try to see eye-to-eye with our partners on all matters, we are impeccably empathic and understanding of one another, there are no problems, everything is wonderful, we are always linked energetically, we are indeed blessed, and we do everything together all the time. We put all of our energies into keeping the partnership trouble free and do our best to ignore any feelings of discomfort. The rule we hold in our minds is something like "in a really good relationship, everything runs smoothly, both partners always agree with each other, and they never separate but always do everything together." Unfortunately, when we try to keep the relationship perfect in this way, we actually break the connection between our partners and ourselves because anything that does not work smoothly is ignored and too much gets left out.

Since relationships naturally ebb and flow and life is not always wonderful, perfection is not exactly an attainable objective. As a matter of fact, if this goal is attained and there is never any friction, we might suspect that something is being overlooked. This does not mean that relationships are always a mass of difficulties. What it does mean is (1) people are different and have different needs, (2) two partners invariably experience some areas of disconnection, disagreement, or misunderstanding, and (3) there is always a need for some separation as well as a need for togetherness.

This is why it is so important to be able to include in the partnering relationship some space for the consideration of what is not working, either in the relationship or in your life. If you were running, a business and you never looked at what did not work, you might find yourself in deep trouble. For instance, you run a freight service. Everybody knows that you only like good news, so no one tells you that there is a small knocking sound in the refrigerated truck that does your long-distance runs. If you knew about it, you could have the problem fixed. But you do not find out about it because nobody wants to bring you the bad news and they tell themselves that since it is only a small knocking sound, it is probably not very important. So the truck breaks down in the middle of the desert with a full load of perishable lettuce.

It is the "small knocking sounds" that tell us what could be improved upon, what could grow into a problem, or what needs fixing. We all need time — and permission — to look at what is not working in our lives and in the relationship. In the partnering model of relationship, it is accepted that each partner can, and will, bring to the conference table "reports" of what is not currently working. This is not a gripe session any more than a business meeting to review the workings of a business is a gripe session.

What might you bring to the table? You would bring your dissatisfactions with your partner or your life. This might include talking about your attractions to others, attractions that pull you away from the relationship. You might include your fantasies, such as opening a new business, or having another baby, or running away to Fiji. You might talk of your fears about money, work, health, or even about the relationship. You might talk about your discomfort with always being together and express your need for time alone, or for a space in the house that is just yours. All these issues keep us from becoming too complacent or stuck in old patterns that no longer suit us; they all open doors into new thoughts and new possibilities.

We feel that it is important to have time set aside to look at these matters. It is not necessary to be formal about this — after all you are not running a business — but it is important to keep current. Keeping current with dissatisfactions or negative feelings (1) helps us to keep the connection with our partners alive, even if the connection is not pleasant at that very moment, (2) prevents a backlog of complaints from building up, and (3) helps us to deal with matters creatively and quickly. We fix the truck before it breaks down. That is what partners are for.

Each partner notices something different and contributes something unique to the partnership. You may become irritated when your partner gets too preoccupied with work and ignores you. Your partner may become irritated with you because you did not follow up on the business opportunity that presented itself last week. You may be great at noticing when the car needs repairing and your partner may be great at noticing when the bank accounts are getting too low. You can see how partnering as a model for relationship brings us the possibilities of using our full human potential as a powerful team.

MEETING THE CHALLENGES

The basic theme in all ten challenges is the underlying challenge to maintain the connection in your primary relationship. Most of the time this connection will be pleasant, but there are times, when you are dealing with unpleasant matters, when it will be a bit uncomfortable.

What must you do on a day-to-day basis to maintain the connection to your partner? First, you must make your relationship — and this connection — a priority. All the challenges mentioned in this chapter have a single common element. Each of them threatens to replace your relationship as a priority.

Second, when you feel uncomfortable with your partner or the relationship, or when you sense your connection weakening, don't ignore your feelings. This is a warning, it is like a fire alarm going off. You may be tempted to think that the alarm is faulty and you may wish to turn if off because you can't bear the sound, you don't see any smoke, and you're too busy to go looking for trouble. But pay attention. There is a gift of disowned energy somewhere in this discomfort.

The third, and perhaps the most important, ingredient in the recipe for a healthy, intimate, and loving relationship is time. The best way to meet all the challenges to relationship is to take time for one another and for your partnership. You cannot run a business without giving it proper time and attention, and you cannot expect to have a successful relationship without doing likewise. Take time for meetings, for work, for play, and for passion. Take time to be happy with each other and time to be irritated with each other. Take time to look at what works and makes you feel just great and time to listen to the small knocking sounds in your relationship and your lives that will tell you what doesn't work. Take time to enjoy today and time to plan and to dream about tomorrow. Take time to hang out, just to *be* and not to *do* anything at all.

Most of all, take time away from the daily distractions and

challenges we've been talking about to establish and to keep the delicious energetic linkage between you and your partner. It's a good idea to make regular plans to break your daily routine and get re-acquainted. These breaks can take any form, so be creative.

If partners can keep their linkage, they will keep their relationship. Anything that breaks this linkage can damage the relationship. No matter how sensible, worthwhile, or absolutely necessary the distraction seems to be, it should be handled with great care and not allowed to break the essential connection between partners. It is very easy to ruin even a good relationship. It is also very easy, once we know about linkage, to preserve a good relationship and to make it even better. So go for the linkage, and good luck!

Chapter 10

PARTNERS ON THE PATH: SPIRITUALITY AND PARTNERING

The surrender to the process of relationship is at the same time a surrender to spiritual reality. This sense of transcendent reality awakens us to the remarkable intelligence that governs the universe without and within. Once we are connected to this intelligence we discover a third partner in our relationship. The presence of "the third" brings us a deepening of process, an amazingly knowledgeable ally, and a profound sense of peace that comes with knowing that we do not need to do it all by ourselves.

When it comes to partnering, we are not alone. We have our interactions with each other in the partnering relationship and we have something else as well. We have our spiritual reality. As Jewish theologian and philosopher Martin Buber said so beautifully: "There is a light over every person, and when two souls meet, their lights come together, and a single light emerges from them to feel the universal generation as a sea, and oneself as a wave in it."

There are many different ways to think about this. You can call it being connected to God, being connected to universal or transpersonal energies, or being connected to the intelligence of the universe that echoes within each of us. You can also think of it as the impulse in us that wishes to serve our fellow humans and to make the planet a better place. However you choose to frame the spiritual aspect of life, it is real, it is objective, and it is essential for our individual well-being, the well-being of our partnering relationship, and the well-being of the planet.

For us it is clear that there is in the universe, and within each of us, a deeper intelligence that can be ignited as we begin our journey of personal discovery. Once this intelligence is activated it has the possibility of becoming an always-available friend and teacher to us. And what a remarkable friend and teacher it can be! With its help, we begin to make sense out of things that were previously a mass of confusion. We experience meaning, purpose, and direction in our personal lives that simply were not there before. Our dreams begin to make sense to us and they become an important part of our lives. New thoughts, new ways of looking at things emerge.

As we plug into this newly developing intelligence, we begin to experience the meaning and purpose that lie behind it. It wants something from us. It drives us with inexorable power and certainty toward a deeper understanding of our relationships and ourselves. It replaces in importance many of the other concerns in our lives. Our belief systems and the rules we have lived by in the past are now open to examination and a deeper consideration. We feel the purposive nature of this intelligence, we know that it wants something from us, and that it is moving us in an entirely new direction.

Our personal view is that this intelligence wishes us to become all that we can be, to make use of everything that we brought with us into this world. It wants us to embrace all of our selves so that we can more fully enter into life and relationship and learn to balance the remarkable array of energies that are within us. It wants us to claim our full humanity.

It is a source of immense strength (and a relief, too, we might add) to experience divinity as an integral part of one's partnering relationship. Life in general, and relationship in particular, can be pretty rough going at times. In their groundbreaking book, *Flesh and Spirit,* Jack Zimmerman, Ph.D., and Jaquelyn McCandless, M.D., write about "the third" in relationship. They point out the need to always call in "the third" so that divinity is present and available to us, not just for our individual lives but also for our relationships. This third is an important part of what makes relationship sacred.

What must we do to begin to connect to this divine intelligence? Sometimes we do not have to do anything. Just beginning the process of personal growth can activate this intelligence. Once it is activated, it is there for us. We just have to know where to look for it. Since there are specific ways in which this intelligence manifests, there are also particular things that we can do to support the connection to this divine intelligence and to enhance the spiritual basis of the partnering process. Let's now look at some of the things that you can do to deepen your connection to yourself and to your partnering.

DREAMS AS A WINDOW TO YOUR INNER SELVES AND SPIRITUALITY

Perhaps the simplest, the most fascinating, and the most rewarding place to begin is with dreams. Our dreams give us the most direct experience of this deeper intelligence. They also bring us into connection with our own spiritual reality, a reality that, of others.

Your dreams can help you understand the amazing family of selves that lives within you. Your dreams are remarkable friends; they give you an objective, or unbiased, picture of how your selves dance with each other and, we might add, dance with the selves of your partner. Let's look at the dream process and see what it can teach you about these selves.

We know that there are many useful ways of looking at dreams. You may have studied dreams already and have your own inter-pretations. The following is our own particular approach to dream work, one that we have found extremely helpful over the years. As you read this, remember that each of us has our own dream vocab-ulary, so please be aware that yours may be a bit different from this in some places.

Common Themes in Dreams

There are some dream themes that are very common. We will begin by looking at these and showing you (1) how you might decode them and (2) how you can use the information that they are bringing you.

High Places

Dreaming of being in a high place takes many forms. Sometimes the dreamer is on top of a tall building or on a high mountaintop. There is often a danger of falling, or at least there is some sense that a person in this situation could fall. In some of these dreams, the dreamer is in fact falling from a high place.

When you are up high you are away from the earth. You might be too identified with your mind or with spirituality, which indi-cates that either your rational mind or your spiritual self is likely functioning as your primary self. You are probably disconnected from earth and all that it represents. This would mean that you dis-own your body, your feelings, or your instinctual energies. Another way of looking at this kind of dream is that people who are spe-cial, and who disown the ordinary, are always high up. Their posi-tion is precarious because whenever they stop being special, they can fall down and they fear that when they fall down they will become nothing.

We keep falling in our dreams because we continue to remain

too identified with our minds, our being special, or our spiritual nature. So the unconscious shows us falling from high places over and over again. It is basically showing us where we are (up) and what we are missing (down). It is as simple and clear as that. Carl Jung, founder of analytical psychology, called this the compensatory principle of the dream process because the dream is always balancing out whatever we are identified with or whatever we disown.

Fast Cars and Freeways

In these dreams we are driving too fast or our car is out of control. There is often an accident or a crash of some kind.

Driving too fast is the classic dream of a pusher primary self, one that is out of control. The crash stops us. For example, Sonny, a very successful financier, dreams repetitively for many years that he is driving on a freeway at high speeds and his car crashes. This is an accurate picture of the way he actually leads his life. He is always busy and never slows down. After a number of years Sonny has a heart attack. Pusher energy can be very dangerous and this amazing intelligence within was sending him repeated warnings of this danger. (His wife was also telling him he should slow down, but that is another story.) If he had listened to his dream, Sonny would have understood its warning and he would have had the opportunity to separate from his pusher self before he actually got sick.

The car image often gives us a general picture of how we move through the world. If in a dream you are driving the car you drove in college, then your general psychology now is like it was then. If you are in a car and your father is driving it, then your life is being run by your father (either your real father, or the primary self in you that resembles your father).

In these dreams, you are usually racing on a freeway. Again, this is a pusher motif. You might find that, as you pay attention to your dreams and you separate from your pusher, you are now driving down country roads, or you have pulled off the freeway to stop.

Quicksand or Sticky Asphalt

Dreaming that you are trying to walk but it feels like your feet are in quicksand or sticky asphalt is another kind of pusher dream. Here the dream is balancing, or compensating, your primary self, the self that tries to push so hard all the time. Dreams often try to balance our primary self in this way. Here you are trying to hurry and you cannot. Your feet are stuck. The harder you try to reach your destination, the worse things get. Your dream is intent on getting the message through to you. A variation of this dream is one in which you are trying to catch a train or bus or ship and, no matter how hard you try to make it on time, you are too late.

School or Military Service

Dreaming you are back in school or military service is a very common dream. Generally it describes the fact that we are living our life today the way we did when we were in school or in the army. In these settings our lives were not our own and we had to dance to a drumbeat that was not our own. In these settings we had to do what was assigned to us. It is very easy to fall into life patterns that are psychologically very much like being in school or in the army. This dream usually means that we are following a set of rules and requirements that deny us our freedom. We have no choice but are at the mercy of the rules that in this case are usually the rules of a particularly demanding set of primary selves.

A variation of this dream is being in prison or being locked up in a concentration camp. These dreams reflect a loss of personal freedom in our lives and often indicate a lack of connection to our feelings. They usually come when we are working too hard and life is becoming a prison.

Police Officers

The police represent control. Very often when the pusher energy is out of control in our lives, we have dreams of a police officer stopping us for a traffic violation. This dream is also a compensatory dream. There is something in your life that is out of control and your control side is trying to help you regain control and, most likely, trying to get you to slow down. These are warning dreams and you need to learn to listen to them.

Houses

There are very many variations on the house dream. The image of the home represents your personality and how it is operating in the world. The house gives you a picture of how you are living. Is there enough space? Is there enough light? Is it cold? Is it magical? Do you have your own special space? Dreaming of moving into a new home is connected to a major change in personality. Many times when people are bringing more choice into their lives, they dream of new and more spacious houses.

Sometimes people dream that they are going down into the basement, where they feel fearful. In this case they are moving more deeply into the unconscious as they explore new aspects of themselves. Discovering new rooms or new treasures in a house is learning about new parts of yourself. Dreaming of living in a Victorian-type home might be related to having a set of primary selves that is based on Victorian values.

Dangerous People or Things

Being chased by dangerous people or things is one of the most common types of dreams. *Whatever is chasing you in your dreams is essentially based on what you are disowning.* Many people disown their instinctual energies. They are afraid of their anger, their sexuality, or their emotions. So in their dreams they are chased by wild animals or by dangerous men who want to kill them or have sexual relations with them. By examining what is after you in your dreams, you have immediate access to discovering your disowned selves!

Sometimes these disowned selves can represent parts of ourselves other than our instinctual energies. If you are a pusher type bent on success, then you may find yourself afraid of people who are not busy, like unemployed street people, people in hammocks, or "ladies who lunch." We saw a woman once who dreamed a dragon was chasing her. She crossed a small body of water and there the dragon stopped and became a book. She was a woman who had disowned the serious use of her mind and that became the dragon that was after her. A few months after this dream she enrolled in school and ultimately pursued a professional career.

Birth and Death

The unconscious needs a way to describe change in our personality development. The image of people giving birth to babies is a wonderful way to describe the development of new ideas, new feelings, and new ways of being in the world.

Conversely, the image of someone dying is a way of describing the end of a certain cycle, the end of a certain way of thinking or feeling or being in the world. There is a Buddhist saying that life is a thousand births and a thousand deaths, and when we look at the frequency of the birth and death motif in dreams, we can certainly see how this is true.

If you dream that you die it is generally a time of great change in your life. In these situations you are usually shifting away from your primary self system. It is like a death. The old you is dying and a new you will be born.

Cataclysms

There are a wide variety of cataclysmic dreams. These suggest that there is a big change coming. Here are some of them: There is a huge earthquake and you know that it is the end of the world. It is World War III and you know that the world is coming to an end. There is a gigantic tidal wave that is going to destroy everything.

In most of these dreams the dreamer is going to die. Keep in mind that the dreamer in the dream is generally one of your primary selves. Dreaming of a tidal wave may suggest that your disowned emotional selves are getting ready to overwhelm your rational, controlled primary self. An earthquake means that your primary self that had everything in order is about to be overturned.

Flying (Not in a Plane)

This is also a very common kind of dream. To make sense out of it we have to determine the primary self of the dreamer. If someone is a very concrete thinker and a practical person with a strong attention to detail, then the dream reflects a readiness to move into his or her intuition, into the world of the imagination, and, very possibly, into the spiritual sphere.

If, on the other hand, the dreamer is very much identified with intuition and spirituality, then the dream can reflect an overidentification with intuition and the spiritual world. It means that the dreamer is always up in the air and does not have his or her feet on the ground.

Sometimes you are being chased in a dream or a situation is extremely emotional and then you jump up and start to fly. This would be a reflection of moving into fantasy to escape a situation that is too difficult to handle on a psychological level.

DREAMS AND RELATIONSHIP

So far we have been discussing certain categories of dreams that give us pictures of ourselves and the way in which we are living our lives. You can see, as we study these dreams, that we have a friend inside of us, a kind of dream master. This dream master, who is really the intelligence of the unconscious manifesting itself in the dream process, is an amazing adviser. It brings us all kinds of information, ideas, insights, and new ways of looking at things. It seems to want us to look at and embrace more and more of what we are. Its insights about relationship are staggering.

The Psychological Divorce

Listen to the following dream of a woman who had come to one of our workshops with her husband. They had both begun to separate from rigidly controlling primary selves and were beginning to meet each other in an entirely new, far more flexible way. This was her dream the last night of the training:

People are waiting for me to come down to the wedding ceremony except that it was actually a divorce ceremony. I'm wearing the same dress as the wedding dress I wore to my actual wedding. The bodice of this dress is different, however. It is beautiful with colored beads across it. Neither of us has the script quite ready and so we are not quite ready for the ceremony to begin.

This is a remarkable dream. What is this divorce ceremony the couple is about to go through? It is the divorce from their primary selves. We think of it as a psycho-spiritual divorce, something that every couple truly needs. It marks the end of the relationship between two primary selves and the beginning of a relationship between two complex, sentient, soulful partners.

Many years ago Hal dreamed that he was in a court of law standing before a judge. The judge asked him what he was there for and Hal told him that he wanted a divorce from his wife (Sidra). The judge then asked Hal why he wanted this divorce and Hal told him that he wanted it because he loved her so much!

At that particular time Hal was learning to separate from the good father and the responsible father, the primary selves that had been so dominant in his life. Both of these selves had bonded him to Sidra in a way that worked against a deepening of the relationship. So long as Hal was identified with his good father, he could not react properly to Sidra, nor could he establish appropriate boundaries for himself. With the divorce from his primary selves —

and from the bonding patterns — he was released and the relationship could move to the next level. This psychological divorce is the divorce that all partners must ultimately get from each other. It is the one that really counts.

Bringing Vulnerability into the Relationship

Let's look at another example of how the dream process can point the way in relationship. A physicist came to see us. He was married to an artist, his total opposite in every way. Try as they might, they could not get close to one another. He had no connection to his feelings and his vulnerability. Needless to say, these were her strong suit. During one of our workshops he had the following dream:

I'm walking down a road and I hear someone crying. I look to see where it is coming from. I walk to the side of the road and there I see a hand sticking up from the earth. I rush over and start to dig. When I finally dig deeply enough, I discover a very young child and I pull him out of the earth.

Who is this young child that he discovers, that he is ready to discover? It is himself as a four-year-old when he had to "bury" his vulnerability. The dream master is giving him a picture of his own feeling nature that was buried at that time because his family was too disturbed and he needed to protect himself. He developed a strong logical mind that figured things out. With this, he felt safe no matter how much emotional disturbance surrounded him.

No wonder the physicist and his wife had such difficulty relating. To live in relationship without vulnerability is to live in torment because there is no place to touch at that deeper level that can provide the real food for the soul.

The Dream Master's Picture of the Relationship

Sometimes the dream master of the unconscious uses humor to describe what is happening in a relationship. Many years ago, we got into quite a negative place with each other. It was pretty grim. Hal went into negative father mode and began taking potshots at Sidra for much of the day and into the evening. These took the form of constant criticisms that she blithely sidestepped. That night Sidra had the following dream:

> *Hal is throwing lit matches at me. I keep dodging them so he cannot hit me. Finally Hal explodes and yells at me: "Stop jumping around so much. Stand still so that I can hit you."*

When we woke up the next morning and Sidra shared her dream, we both started laughing. The unconscious had made its statement and it was very difficult for Hal to stay locked into the negative energy any longer. We cannot tell you how many times in our life together a dream, or a combination of our dreams, has broken a negative bonding pattern between us. What a gift!

Sometimes the directness of the unconscious is quite extreme when it wants us to get the picture of what is happening in the relationship. In one instance, a woman dreamed that her husband was having an affair with another woman. She felt it was a dream so she did not say anything and the next night she had the same dream. Then, amazingly enough, the dream repeated itself a third time.

On the morning after the third dream the woman asked her husband at breakfast if he was having an affair. Once he got over the shock, he admitted to her that such was the case and they began to deal with their relationship and its problems. Imagine the intelligence of the dream master who insisted, who demanded, that this woman become conscious of this affair so that she could meet the challenge and move on with her life and deepen her process. It is as though the dream master forces us to shed our skin over and over again so that change can occur. For anyone who works with dreams, the hand of God is patently obvious and truly inspiring.

Another woman was married to a man who saw himself as very spiritual. He meditated a good deal and often criticized his wife because she did not meditate or have a spiritual practice of any kind. You might say that he was spiritually arrogant. During the course of one of our trainings, the wife had the following dream:

I am standing in a line of people next to an altar. Each person has a gift to bring to God that they place on the altar one by one. Many of the gifts are beautifully wrapped. All I have is a pile of loose gunk in my hand. The gunk is all of the confusion and problems of my life. It is loose and I can hardly hold it in my hand. I feel so very ashamed that this is all I have. Finally it is my turn and I place the gunk on the altar, where it quickly spreads all over. Then, from above, a large fist comes down into the middle of the gunk and suddenly the gunk begins to solidify and out of it emerges a large fish. It is given to me as a gift and I am meant to eat it.

What a remarkable gift the dream master brought to this woman. She never thought of herself as being spiritual. It was her husband who knew how to do that. Suddenly everything was framed in a different way. There was a meaning in her life. Her problems were not just problems. They were the substance of her own transformation. Her dream was a dream for all of us. It showed her that God lives here, now, with all of our problems and all of our imperfections. All we need to do is to step to the altar and give to divinity our greatest gift — ourselves with all of our imperfections. You may be sure that a decisive shift occurred in their relationship as a result of this dream and its message.

With another couple the dream master provided another picture. The husband was always complaining about the fact that he felt his wife was overly protected. He wanted to reach her but never could. During one of our trainings she had the following dream:

I dreamed that I was in a large fortress made of concrete. It had thick walls and great battlements. I was snuggled down safe inside of the fortress feeling comfortable and glad that I had its protection all around me. I felt safe and well taken care of. Then I could see outside of my fortress and I saw what it was protecting me from. I saw that it was protecting me from a very soft gentle rain that was falling all around, a rain that would have felt good and would have nurtured me and helped me to grow. I was still glad that I was in my fortress, however.

What a remarkable picture of herself the dream master brings to her. Here she is, encased in her fortress. What is outside? A beautiful soft gentle rain that can nourish her if only she would allow it. Eventually she will leave her fortress but for now she needs this protection. What is the fortress? It is her primary self system. It is her mind, her control, her iron discipline, and her absolute requirement that she show no vulnerability.

So we see how dreams so beautifully reflect the dance of the selves as they operate within us and in our relationships. The dream world is like the handwriting of God. What a creative collaboration it is when partners learn how to decipher this writing with each other. Just telling your dreams to one another is a great way to start. There are many different ways to look at and work with dreams. It does not matter where you begin. Just know that the dream master and the unconscious love attention and they both flower when you spend time with them.

PUSHERS, FREEWAYS, AND THE SOUL

In order to feel our spiritual natures, we need to slow our lives down so we can see and feel and smell and taste what is around us. We often use the image of driving on the freeway to describe the speed and the power of the inner pusher. The pusher is driven by a deep anxiety about life and tries to cope with this anxiety by making us successful and helping us to earn a living. But whatever its motivation, the pusher is merciless in its demands on us and it keeps us moving at extremely high speeds. So one of the things we must learn is how to get off the freeway and begin to drive the country roads of our psyches.

With some couples, both people are so busy that they do not even know that they are no longer making contact with each other. Many years ago Hal saw a child in therapy who drew a picture of his family home. In the picture some people were racing up and down stairs while others were moving sideways, as though they were on wheels. Everyone was going so fast that no one was making contact with anyone else. That is how the pusher operates. You may get a good deal of work done and you may set new speed records, but you can forget intimacy and linkage and you most assuredly can forget about matters of the spirit.

Spiritual teachers will frequently recommend meditation as a way of slowing down and accessing spirit. We have no objection to meditation used for this purpose, and it often works. The difficulty is that this does not solve the fundamental problem of a hyperactive pusher. It merely gives the meditator a break.

Imagine for a moment that you are driving on the autobahn at 120 miles per hour. It is now meditation time. You slam on the brakes and pull over and meditate for a half hour. Well that is certainly better than not meditating at all, but what happens when the meditation is over? You are back on the autobahn traveling 120 miles per hour, or maybe 130 miles per hour since you may feel you have to make up the time you lost while you were stopped.

The challenge to individuals and the challenge to partners is to meet this pusher energy together and find a way to slow down the car. We need to learn to build into our life times to be still or to move slowly and ways of being still or of moving with stillness. It is when we are still that we make our deeper and more intimate connections to each other and to the world of the spirit.

If we cannot learn how to do this on a psychological level, then drugs and alcohol become the method of choice for many of us. They do slow us down temporarily. They also shut down the cacophony of voices in our heads, especially the self-critical one who, together with the pusher, does so much to exhaust us and distress us and to maintain the success of the psychotherapy and medical professions.

GETTING OFF THE FREEWAY: LINKAGE AND THE EXPERIENCE OF SPIRIT

When you learn to quiet down and *be* with each other, a very remarkable thing can happen. We are not talking now about watching TV together or reading together. Those are parallel activities in which both partners are still *doing* something. We are talking now about sitting opposite each other all alone with no one else around and simply exchanging energy.

We usually prefer no talking for five or ten minutes and minimal talking during the remainder of these times together. Just *be* together with no agenda and no expectations. You might want to play quiet music, but it should not be music that enlivens and distracts, it should be music that quiets and deepens. As far as we are concerned, *this is sacred time and it is a time when spirit can enter and soul reality can make its essential meaning known.*

This also is not a time for sexuality. That does something else for intimacy between partners. Some people use sexual practices such as those described in the Tantric scriptures to bring the experience of soul into their relationships. However, we have found that the deep intimacy reached during sex does not necessarily carry over to everyday life and partners who achieve intimacy in this way can be as cut off from one another as any other couple once the intimate sexual experience is finished. Physical intimacy does not in any way ensure a real intimacy and linkage. But it certainly can contribute!

We can only ask you to spend some time just quietly *being* together and see what happens. You can develop your own way of doing this. Just keep it simple since this is a time for *being* and not for *doing*. The gift of linkage and the gift of spirit in relationship are priceless and well worth the effort.

GROUP ACTIVITIES THAT SUPPORT SPIRITUAL CONTACT

There are many kinds of group activities that support the experience of spiritual energies. A group of people who focus on bringing in spiritual energies can command a great deal of authority and catch the attention of the higher order energies. You may wish to join a traditional church or synagogue if this works for you. It may be a workshop or class where spirituality is taught and inducted. It may be just a group of people who gather to meet, travel, meditate, or pray.

In the wonderful Kevin Costner film *Field of Dreams,* the character that Costner plays is told by the voice in the field: "If you build it, they will come!" In the film this voice turns out to be that of his departed father. We say to you the same thing. If you make the time and space for them and call them (or him or her or it), they will come. We are talking about the presence of divine energy. If more than one person, such as a group, calls, the energies that come in are even more immediate and more powerful.

In the fall of 1998, we traveled to Bhutan with some good friends. It was a magical, spirit-infused time. There were six of us altogether: Joseph Heller, Kathleen Downes, Lynnaea Lumbard, Rick Paine, and ourselves. We meditated and prayed together in many of the Buddhist temples and the ancient shrines in Bhutan. The experience was a remarkable one for all of us. The two of us alone would have had a good time but we could not have begun to approach the level of intensity that occurred over and over again during these group meditations.

RITUAL ACTIVITY AND SACRED SPACE

One of the very lovely things that we have done is to create rituals in our life together aimed at being related to the world of spirit or asking it for help in some way. For example, each morning Sidra lights an oil lamp and incense in front of the Thai spirit house in our kitchen and when we leave on a long trip Hal lights incense in the front and rear gardens while Sidra lights the incense and oil lamp inside.

We have arranged sacred spaces in our home and in the garden. These are like small temple areas or altars. You can do whatever you like to create your own. Many people have a sacred space for their meditation practice. Outdoor spaces may involve arrangements of statues, stones, wood, and plants. Inside they can be sacred spaces — or altars — where you keep all sorts of special objects or photos in an attractive arrangement. You can use these sacred spaces for lighting candles or burning incense.

On a few occasions we have taken off our wedding bands and buried them in the earth for a period of time and then put them back on, each placing the ring on the other's finger as we did during our original wedding ceremony. We have spoken new vows to each other on a number of occasions as a renewal of our connection. We often pray together, more as a ritual than as a regular ongoing activity.

Most people are bashful about their feelings toward God. So we say to you that if you are bashful, be bashful. Just do not let it stop you from doing what you need to do or say to feel connected to the world of spirit. Do not get cerebral and worry so much about details, like whether God is male or female, that you stop your own prayer and ritual. There is nothing wrong with religious speculation and thought so long as it does not take the juice out of your own brand of practice and ritual. Do whatever feels right to you. This is primarily a matter of heart and soul.

THE HAND OF GOD IN RELATIONSHIP

It is in our study of relationship that we have been the most moved, the most touched by what we see as the hand of divinity. The intelligence of the universe has created such an amazing system for becoming conscious that we stand in awe, over and over again, as we observe couples learning to become partners and claiming what they need to claim. The deep joys of these relationships and the rewards of this partnering are so marvelous that they feel like gifts from God.

We have learned that there are two basic laws of relationship. The first is the law of the disowned selves. Whatever it is that you hate or judge or cannot stand in the world is your disowned self. If you hate your partner's neatness and you constantly feel judgment, then neatness is a disowned self. If your partner cannot bear it when you flirt at a party, then flirting is your partner's disowned self.

We can even take this a step further. It is not just what you judge that is a disowned self, it is whatever destabilizes you. If you are excessively jealous of your sister because she is so sexy, then sexiness is a disowned self. If you are powerfully attracted to a teacher that you met, then your disowned self will be your own inner teacher or your own spiritual nature or whatever it is that he or she teaches.

It is not just the law itself that is so profound for us, it is the fact that it behaves with such mathematical precision. As we watch disowned selves at work in the world, as we watch the way the universe sends them back to us like heat seeking missiles (which is what they become when they are disowned), there is no question in our minds any longer that God is truly a mathematician.

The second law, which shows this divine mathematics so beautifully, is as follows: Whatever you disown in your life, whatever self or energy you have repressed, that same self will find you. You will marry that self or your first or second child will embody that self. Your coworker, mother-in-law, dog, cat, ex-spouse, or stepchildren will embody that self. Whenever you are at war with anyone in your life where judgment and negativity are involved, you are dealing with a disowned self.

If you have disowned your vulnerability then one of your children will become ultimately vulnerable. You will either be totally upset with that child or irrevocably bonded to him or her. This will go on all your life together until you recognize that this child is your teacher and you must take back what is yours. In this case it would be your vulnerability. The wicked stepmother that you hate is your deepest teacher. She carries your ability to be unaffected by the needs of others, your impersonality, your ability to use power, and your strategic thinker. So long as you remain angry with her, you keep yourself unconscious and so stop yourself from embracing the missing selves that she carries.

What a remarkable thing the intelligence of the universe has done! What a method it has developed to force us to become more conscious human beings. Is it any wonder that we are filled with awe as we see these immutable laws of the universe applied to relationship?

When looked at in this way, spiritual reality lives in your every moment with people. Your deepest hatred can change suddenly into the most profound experience of divinity and with that experience of divinity comes an effortless compassion and a feeling of deep peace. All that you need do is recognize that your partner is your teacher and commit yourself to doing the work that has to be done. In partnering we make this commitment. Ultimately we will all be moving in this direction. There is nowhere else to go!

Afterword

THE STAR MAIDEN'S BASKET

As we sit here looking out the window at the full moon rising above the eucalyptus trees that protect us from the winter storms, we feel blessed by life and by love. It is spring and the daffodils are in bloom. This is a magical time, the beginning of the last year of this millennium, a time of endings and beginnings.

By the time you read this, it will be the twenty-first century. We are sending you a message from the twentieth and inviting you to learn from those who have gone before. It has not always been an easy path for us and it has not always been an easy path for those who have followed us. We know that relationships are complex and far from easy. They take work. There are many challenges and there is a great deal to learn in order to meet these challenges. But a few laughs along the way help a lot and, in the end, it is worth all the trouble.

At this time in our lives we have experienced much. We have been privileged to accompany many people on their journeys of relationship. We have seen much sadness and pain, but we have

239

also seen wondrous joy and the deepest love. It is really possible to partner one another, to keep your love alive, and to bring in the divine. We would like to assure you that the Star Maiden's basket is not empty!

ACKNOWLEDGMENTS

It has been many years since we started this journey together. We have traveled far and met countless wonderful people who supported us and taught our work. Some are still with us and some have gone their own ways, but we would like to take this opportunity to thank them all and to acknowledge their contributions. We have tried to remember everyone and we hope that we have succeeded.

In the United States we would like to thank Paul Abell, Karen Atwood, Carol Bardin, BearHeart, Harriet Benjamin, Richard Berger, Ruth Berlin, Bonnie Bernell, Jan and Laren Beys, Phil Bohnert, Betty Bosdell, Lucia Capacchione, Dorsey Cartwright, Sindona Cassteel, Tracey Coddington, Alan Cooke, John Cooper, Mary Disharoon, John and LeAnne Dougherty, Miriam Dyak, Susan Filley, JoAnne Gaffney, James Gagner, Elizabeth Gawain, Jonathon Goodman-Herrick, Judy Harlan, Judith Hendin, Lisa Hughes, Essie Hull, Anna Ivara, Nicolee Jikyo, Catherine Keir, Christien King, Yolanda Koumidou, Arianne Koven, Alex Lessin, Arthur Levy, John Livingstone, Lynnaea Lumbard, Tanha Luvaas, Gloria Manon, Sharon Steele McGee, Ed Moffett, Deborah Morris, Eric Morris,

Randy Morris, Regina WaterSpirit Newell, Brooks and Rod Newton, Larry Novick, Lora O'Connor, Janny Padelford, J'aime Ona Pangaia, Francine Pinto, Abby Rosen, Elaine Rosenson, Kathleen Rountree, Alice Scully, Marsha Sheldon, Susan Sims Smith, Francesca Starr, William Taegel, Manuela TerraLuna, Jennifer Walton, Jane Winters, Marta Lou Wolff, Annette Woods, and Judith Yost.

Our teaching in Holland goes back to 1981 and we would like to give special thanks to the original two teachers, Robert Stamboliev and Jerien Koolbergen. Robert has introduced our work in a number of other countries in Europe, in Scandinavia, Russia, and even Réunion Island. There are many others in Holland who have supported us and our work, including Maria Daniels, Berenda Dekkers, Peter Dellensen, David Grabjin, Wendy Hobbelink, Alfredo Leewis, Hermien Mensink, Lex Mulder, Joke van der Niet, Lietje Perizonius, Marian van Riemsdijk, and Trilby Fairfax Shaw.

Since our first visit to Australia in 1987, there have been many fine people who welcomed us and supported our work. We would like to extend special thanks to Lydia Duncan, who first introduced us to Australia, and to Robin and Paul Gale-Baker, who have not only supported and taught the work but also distribute our books and tapes Down Under. Michael and Paulina Rowland and John Coroneos have worked tirelessly to produce a series of teaching videotapes of this work. Thanks are also due to Ana Barner, Lorraine Benham, Sandy Beswarick, Thalia Castles, Leni Foster, Valma Granich, Liz Greene, Diane Hinder-Hawkins, Susie Itzstein, Susan James, Bruce Jenkins, Debbie Joffe, Mary King, Astra Neidra, Victoria Resch, Diana Scambler, Paul Sheriff, John Sinclair, and John Swinburne.

In Canada we'd like to extend a special thank-you to Anne Kerr Linden who introduced our work in Toronto. We are also grateful for the ongoing support we have received from Mary Barrett, Greg Heraldson, Karinna and Tom James, Mary Langley, Donna Quance, and Roger Rolfe.

We would like to say a special thank-you to Artho Wittemann

and Veeta Gensberger, who supported our work with such enthusiasm. They introduced our work into Germany, supervised the translation and publication of the books in German, and have incorporated our work into theirs. Also, a thank-you to Tilke Plateel and Richard Lamm, who originally taught our work in Holland and are now teaching in Germany.

Our thanks to the group in Sweden including Onya Dowling, Leela Jansson, Franciska von Koch, Frans Kochen, and Jacques Laurent. It has been a pleasure to work with all of you.

We are grateful to Monique Assal, Yael Haft (formerly of Israel), Joy Manné, Adelheid Oesch, and Eberhard Winkler, who have welcomed this work into Switzerland.

In England, our thanks go to Helen de Castre, Naomi Cotton, Lorna Knox, Gabriella Pinto, Lee Preisler, Toni Tye, and Esther Zahniser for their continuing support.

We are very appreciative of the many contributions of the teachers in France, Véronique Brard, Geneviève Cailloux, Pierre Cauvin, Diana Smith, and Angela Vona, and would like to thank them for their support and enthusiasm. We'd like to add an extra thank-you to Véronique Brard for her help with translation and publication.

Our friend and colleague Susan Schwartz Senstad originally introduced this work in Norway and has expanded it into business and government. Our special thanks to Liv Dons Samset for her help with the translation and publication of our books in Norwegian.

We have fond memories of our work in Mexico and would like to thank Olga Salas Portugal for arranging everything and Graciela Delhumeau and Eva Somlo for their efforts on behalf of this work.

Many thanks to Franca Errani for her inspired teaching in Italy and for her careful work with the translation of our books into Italian. In Luxembourg, our thanks to Christian Sarti for his support.

Fr. Bill Whittier has traveled the world as an emissary and introduced our work to such places as Ireland, India, and Africa. We are particularly grateful that he has given us the opportunity to touch many lives that we otherwise would never have reached.

We never could have done all of this without the people who have helped us manage the details of the office and our workshops. We'd like to extend special thanks to Penny Ayeroff, Susie Farrar, Launa Marlo, and Marilyn Reardon for all they gave to us in the past. As for the present, we just couldn't get everything done without Anne Kight, Stephanie Berry, and last, but certainly not least, our office manager, Marilou Brewer!

To Marc Allen of New World Library and Shakti Gawain of Nataraj Publishing, who encouraged us to write this book, thanks for your support and your continuing commitment to our work. To Gina Misiroglu, our magnificent editor, we say thank you for all your help and your enthusiasm. It has been great working with you.

There are some very special people in our lives who have journeyed with us for many years and are major teachers of our work. These are Hal's daughter Judith Stone and our dear friends Carolyn Conger, Lydia Duncan, Shakti Gawain, Joseph Heller, and Dassie Hoffman.

Our families have provided us with much richness and love, great gifts, and major lessons in life. We are deeply grateful to be related to Elizabeth, Claudia, Recha, Judith, and Joshua, to Dave, Jon, and Wistancia, and to Haley, Rachel, and Jake.

Photograph by Sam Young

ABOUT THE AUTHORS

Hal Stone, Ph.D., and Sidra Stone, Ph.D., are the creators of Voice Dialogue and the authors of (among others) the trailblazing books *Embracing Our Selves, Embracing Each Other,* and *Embracing Your Inner Critic.* Their books have been translated into Danish, Dutch, French, German, Italian, Norwegian, and Swedish.

For the past eighteen years, Hal and Sidra have taught together, both nationally and internationally, on the subjects of voice dialogue, relationship and the selves, and the psychology of the aware ego. They have led workshops in Australia, Canada, England, Holland, France, Germany, Norway, Israel, Hungary, Mexico, and Switzerland. They are inspired teachers who bring to their work humor, enthusiasm, and a very practical and earthy approach to the transformational process.

Hal and Sidra are both licensed clinical psychologists with many years of professional experience as psychotherapists. In addition to this, Hal, originally trained as a Jungian analyst, founded the Center for the Healing Arts in Los Angeles in the early 1970s. This center was a prototypical holistic health center and one of the first to emphasize illness as a path for spiritual growth. During those years, Sidra was the executive director of Hamburger Home, a therapeutically oriented residential treatment center for adolescent girls.

As for their personal experience, Hal and Sidra have walked many different paths in their lives in a variety of settings. Hal was originally born in Detroit and Sidra in Brooklyn, but they lived most of their adult lives in Los Angeles. They currently live in Mendocino County on the fog-shrouded coast of Northern California. Between them, they have five grown children and three grandchildren.

BOOKS AND TAPES BY
HAL STONE AND SIDRA STONE

Books

*Embracing Our Selves**

Hal Stone, Ph.D. and Sidra Stone, Ph.D.

*Embracing Each Other**

Hal Stone, Ph.D. and Sidra Stone, Ph.D.

Embracing Your Inner Critic

Hal Stone, Ph.D. and Sidra Stone, Ph.D.

You Don't Have to Write a Book

Hal Stone, Ph.D. and Sidra Stone, Ph.D.

Embracing Heaven and Earth

Hal Stone, Ph.D.

*The Shadow King**

Sidra Stone, Ph.D.

Audio Cassette Tapes

Meeting Your Selves

The Dance of the Selves in Relationship

Understanding Your Relationships

The Child Within

The Voice of Responsibility

Meet the Pusher

Meet Your Inner Critic

Meet Your Inner Critic II

The Patriarch Within

Children and Marriage

Affairs and Attractions

Our Lost Instinctual Heritage

The Pleaser

The Rational Mind

The Psychological Knower

Accessing the Spiritual Dimension

Introducing Voice Dialogue

Voice Dialogue Demonstrations

Decoding Your Dreams

Exploring the Dark Side in Dreams

Integrating the Daemonic

Visions and Prophecies

On Aging

Reflections at Sixty-Five

Audio Cassette Sets

The Aware Ego

*The Mendocino Series: Voice Dialogue, Relationship, and
    the Psychology of Selves*

Making Relationships Work for You

Making Your Dreams Work for You

Videocassettes

The Total Self

The Inner Critic in Action

Ending the Tyranny of the Inner Patriarch

The Voice Dialogue Series (Twelve tape documentary)

*These items are available through New World Library
Phone: (800) 972-6657 (Ext. 52) / Fax: (415) 884-2199
E-mail: escort@nwlib.com
Web site: www.nwlib.com

For all other items and workshop information, contact:
Delos, Inc.
Phone: (707) 937-2424 / Fax: (707) 937-4119
E-mail: delos@mcn.org
Web site: www.delos-inc.com

ADDITIONAL RESOURCES

Dyak, Miriam. *The Voice Dialogue Facilitator's Handbook & Kit.* Seattle, WA: L.I.F.E. Energy Press, 1999.

Gray, John. *Men Are from Mars, Women Are from Venus.* New York: HarperCollins, 1992.

McCandless, Jaquelyn, M.D. and Jack Zimmerman, Ph.D. *Flesh and Spirit.* Las Vegas, NV: Bramble Books, 1998.

Shamboliev, Robert. *The Energetics of Voice Dialogue.* Mendocino, CA: LIFERHYTHM, 1992.

Van der Post, Laurens. *The Heart of the Hunter.* New York: Harcourt Brace Jovanovich, 1980.

If you enjoyed *Partnering,* we recommend the following books and cassettes from New World Library.

Creative Visualization by Shakti Gawain. The classic work (in print for twenty years, three million copies sold) that shows us how to use the power of our imagination to create what we want in life. Available on audio as well, in two formats: the complete book on tape and selected meditations from the book.

Letters to My Son by Kent Nerburn. This is a powerful collection of beautifully crafted letters on life's toughest questions that celebrated author Kent Nerburn wrote to guide his son into adulthood. In this newly revised edition, Nerburn extends his horizons with sections on education and learning, sports and competition.

Living in the Light: A Guide to Personal and Planetary Transformation (Revised) by Shakti Gawain, with Laurel King. A newly updated edition of the recognized classic on developing intuition and using it as a guide in living your life.

Living in the Light Workbook (Revised) by Shakti Gawain with Laurel King. Following up her bestseller, *Living in the Light,* Shakti has created a workbook to help us apply these principles to our lives in very practical ways.

Maps to Ecstasy: A Healing Journey for the Untamed Spirit (Revised). By Gabrielle Roth, with John Loudon. A modern shaman shows us how to reconnect to the vital energetic core of our being through dance, song, theater, writing, meditation, and ritual.

The Path of Parenting by Vimala McClure. *The Path of Parenting* offers twelve principles based on ancient Taoist philosophy and t'ai chi to guide parents in developing long-term philosophical roots as well as short-term solutions about how to be a parent. Filled with practical advice and great inspiration.

The Path of Transformation: How Healing Ourselves Can Change the World. By Shakti Gawain. Shakti gave us *Creative Visualization* in the '70s, *Living in the Light* in the '80, and now *The Path of Transformation* for '90s. This book delivers an inspiring and provocative message for the path of true transformation.

The Power of Now by Eckhart Tolle. In *The Power of Now* Tolle shows readers how to recognize themselves as the creators of their own pain, and how to have a pain-free existence by living fully in the present. Accessing the deepest self — the true self — can be learned, he says, by freeing ourselves from the conflicting, unreasonable demands of the mind and living "present, fully, and intensely in the Now."

The Seven Spiritual Laws of Success by Deepak Chopra. A practical guide to the fulfillment of your dreams. An international bestseller, and for a very good reason. Available on audio as well.

Small Graces by Kent Nerburn. *Small Graces* is a journey into the sacred moments that illuminate our everyday lives. In twenty elegant, short pieces, theologian, sculptor, and writer Kent Nerburn celebrates the daily rituals that reveal our deeper truths.

New World Library publishes books and other
forms of communication on the leading edge
of personal and planetary evolution.

Our books and audio and video cassettes
are in bookstores everywhere.
For a catalog of our complete library
of publications, contact:

New World Library
14 Pamaron Way
Novato, CA 94949

Telephone: (415) 884-2100
Fax: (415) 884-2199
Toll free: (800) 972-6657
Catalog requests: Ext. 50
Ordering: Ext. 52

E-mail: escort@nwlib.com
Web site: www.nwlib.com

Here's what critics are saying about
The High Heels Mysteries:

"A saucy combination of romance and suspense that is simply irresistible."
- Chicago Tribune

"Stylish... nonstop action...guaranteed to keep chick lit and mystery fans happy!"
- Publishers' Weekly, starred review

"Smart, funny and snappy… the perfect beach read!"
- Fresh Fiction

"The High Heels Series is amongst one of the best mystery series currently in publication. If you have not read these books, then you are really missing out on a fantastic experience, chock full of nail-biting adventure, plenty of hi-jinks, and hot, sizzling romance. Can it get any better than that?"
- Romance Reviews Today

"(A) breezy, fast-paced style, interesting characters and story meant for the keeper shelf. 4 ½!"
- RT Book Reviews

"Maddie Springer is like a cross between Paris Hilton and Stephanie Plum, only better. This is one HIGH HEEL you'll want to try on again and again."
- Romance Junkies

OTHER BOOKS BY GEMMA HALLIDAY

High Heels Mysteries:
Spying in High Heels
Killer in High Heels
Undercover in High Heels
Alibi in High Heels
Mayhem in High Heels
Fearless in High Heels
Christmas in High Heels (short story)
Sweetheart in High Heels (short story)

Hollywood Headlines Mysteries:
Hollywood Scandals
Hollywood Secrets
Hollywood Confessions

Anna Smith-Nick Dade Thrillers
Play Nice

Young Adult Books
Deadly Cool
Social Suicide

Other Works
Viva Las Vegas
Haunted (novella)
Watching You (short story)
Confessions of a Bombshell Bandit (short story)